The French Revolution
A CONCISE HISTORY

NORMAN HAMPSON

The French Revolution

A CONCISE HISTORY

with 170 illustrations

CHARLES SCRIBNER'S SONS

NEW YORK

To Françoise and Michèle

Frontispiece: Marat acclaimed
by a jubilant crowd

1 3 5 7 9 11 13 15 17 19 I/C 20 18 16 14 12 10 8 6 4 2

Printed in Great Britain   Dec. 17, 1975
Library of Congress Catalog Card Number 74-33925
ISBN 0-684-14302-X

Contents

Preface   6

1 The social origins of the Revolution   9

2 The intellectual origins of the Revolution   37

3 'Bliss was it in that dawn to be alive': 1789   57

4 New wine and old bottles: 87
October 1789–September 1791

5 The breakdown of authority: 105
October 1791–June 1793

6 The triumph of will: 131
June 1793–June 1794

7 The search for stability: 153
June 1794–November 1799

Conclusion   173

Chronology   177

Bibliography   181

List of illustrations   185

Index   190

Preface

Every year French scholars publish more books and articles on the Revolution than on the sixteenth, seventeenth and eighteenth centuries put together. This at least shows that the subject has not lost its interest for historians. It also means that the amount of information available is far beyond the capacity of anyone to assimilate. There is enough to invalidate almost any impressionistic generalization and too much for systematic analysis. Historians can only put forward personal interpretations that fit a fair proportion of what they regard as the most important facts. As perspectives change, every view is challenged and revised. Each generation has a different idea of what the Revolution was about and why it mattered. All seem to agree, though, that it mattered a great deal.

In a short essay of this kind there can be no question of stopping to justify every controversial interpretation or buttress every hypothesis with supporting evidence. What follows is a personal statement rather than a digest of accepted opinion. It is intended for the layman who enjoys reading history rather than for the examinee. Such readers will, I hope, accept the bald statement of my opinions without all the qualifications that would rightly be expected of a more academic work. None of my views is merely arbitrary and all rest on some factual basis, but none is unchallengeable and if I provoke anyone to a refutation I shall have achieved one of my purposes.

Nothing happens in history unless someone makes it happen. The role of individuals is not always obvious in stable societies where policies are often the work of men who, having risen to the top for conventional reasons, behave in the way that society expects. Stable societies impose their own conservative values, and the price of idiosyncrasy is often impotence. Revolutions have their orthodoxy too, but they offer more scope to the ideologist and the buccaneer. When the old rules are discarded there is a brilliant – if often brief – opportunity for the man with a mission. When the old élites are overthrown, careers are opened to the ruthless and resolute. I have therefore tended to emphasize the role of individuals, partly because they were more important than usual and partly because the immense influence of the Revolution outside France is inseparable from the clash of personalities that fascinated both contemporaries and posterity. Unfortunately, the most conspicuous individuals were rarely the most likeable. I should have preferred to pay more attention to those who sacrificed ambition, reward and sometimes life to the service of a revolution that they saw as a means to the regeneration of mankind. One could very well argue that they were the people who mattered, that the achievements of the Revolution were mainly the product of their self-abnegation. Most of them, however, at least as individuals, lie below the water-line of history. If the reader is disappointed by the behaviour of some of the more eminent men, he should remember the extraordinary pressures to which they were subjected, which help to explain what cannot be excused.

Though my conclusions are my own and would often be rejected by other historians, I have built with the bricks that the latter have provided. Anyone who writes about the Revolution is conscious of belonging to a great international family. Like other families, it has its feuds and antipathies, but the whole would be incomplete if any of its members were excluded. To all of them, both personal friends and those known only through print, I should like to offer my thanks.

CHAPTER ONE

The social origins of
the Revolution

The French Revolution had scarcely begun before Frenchmen started to describe the society it had overthrown as the *ancien régime*. Although they underestimated the extent to which old attitudes survived in new disguises they were right to believe that a whole system of social and legal relationships had come to quite an abrupt end. Looking back from almost two hundred years later it is not easy to penetrate this pre-revolutionary world which, in some respects, was closer to ancient Rome than to the civilization of our own day.

Superficially, French and British society had a good deal in common in the eighteenth century. Both were overwhelmingly agrarian. Most people found it hard to feed themselves and there was not much surplus available, either for the growing towns or for the luxuries of a minority. Land was the main source of wealth and the ownership of land was the best means to economic security and social prestige. Most towns existed primarily as markets. Some were also centres of law courts and local government, where the men who mattered most were judges and royal officials. Most industry consisted of handicrafts, often carried on by part-time farmers or their wives and children. Such large-scale enterprises as existed were usually the creation of great landowners and were situated on their estates. The one significant exception to this largely traditional pattern of economic activity, and the main point of growth, was overseas trade. Maritime commerce was expanding very rapidly and Nantes, Bordeaux and Marseilles were the prototypes of a new kind of society whose wealthy merchants were part of an international economic community.

Although France was a rich country by contemporary standards, most of its people could hope for little more than survival. The rapid growth of population in the eighteenth century, unaccompanied by any significant increase in agricultural productivity, put severe pressure on the available land. Many were permanently dependent on charity to remain alive, and a bad harvest threw tens of thousands on the roads in search of relief. Governments did what they could, by time-honoured methods, to keep the markets supplied and to control the price of grain but the country was too big and land communications were too poor for a surplus in one area to be made available in a distant province. Large-scale famines were a thing of the past but the poor lived with the continual threat of dearth.

Opposite Social relations in the countryside; a seigneur visits a substantial tenant farmer

9

The stomach of Paris: les Halles

Paris: the Halle aux Blés, key to the state of grain supplies

VUE DE L'INT.ᴿ DE LA SALLE
DE LA HALLE AU BLED.

Opposite 'The roads here are stupendous works' (Arthur Young)

Overseas trade was the growth
point of the French economy:
view of the port of Bordeaux

The new economy and the old
society: a lady of obvious
wealth choosing from im-
ported products

The game laws made poaching
a profession

13

The *veillée*, when folk-memories filled the long winter nights

Nothing that statesmanship could do made any appreciable difference in the short run. When harvests were bad the maintenance of law and order was a precarious business as vagrants drifted into rural banditry. Violence was also endemic in the poorer quarters of the towns where life was brutal and precarious.

 So much was common to both England and France; but there were many differences between the two countries. One of the most important arose from the fact that the French peasantry owned between a quarter and a third of the soil. In economic terms this was a mixed blessing, since peasant ownership made enclosure and scientific farming very difficult. Few peasants possessed enough land to feed themselves all the year round and most lacked the capital and knowledge to exploit the potential wealth of what they had. Never-theless, the fact of ownership gave them a certain independence. Villages resisted encroachments by their manorial lords, despite the fact that they almost always lost when they resorted to litigation, since both the manorial and the royal courts reflected the viewpoint of the seigneurs. Conditions varied enormously throughout the country; but in many parts manorial dues formed a big enough share of the lord's income for him to prefer legal chicanery and rack-renting to the long-term investment of capital in his land.

French social life differed from that of England in the greater importance attached to the separate identity of the three traditional

Clerical pomp: Monseigneur de Valras

An idyllic view of the village *curé*

Opposite The marquis de
Sourche and his family – *la
douceur de vivre*

Orders. The clergy, or First Estate, had not much in common with
the Anglican Church. Although the French upper clergy were
closely integrated into aristocratic society – thirteen families controlled a quarter of the 130 bishoprics – celibacy reinforced their
collective *esprit de corps*. The Church owned immense estates,
besides drawing a substantial income from tithes. This wealth
provided a firm economic basis for the autonomy of the Gallican
Church. It was exempt from taxation, and its representatives,
meeting in periodic assemblies, voted such subsidies to the king as
they thought fit. The clergy were disciplined in church courts and
the Church was responsible for education, most hospitals and much
poor relief, besides sharing in control of censorship and providing
the main means for the dissemination of information about government policies.

The case of Charles Maurice de Talleyrand offers a good example
of the way things worked. His distinguished birth and connections
made him Agent Général of the clergy at twenty-six, though his
scandalous life prevented his becoming a bishop until the comparatively late age of thirty-four. As Agent Général he defended the
collective interests of the Church against attempts by the secular
courts to encroach on the disciplining of the clergy and efforts of the
Crown and the Princes of the Blood to pry into its wealth. At the
same time he turned to the state to protect the upper clergy against
the claims of the parish priests, and co-operated with the secular
courts in the suppression of blasphemous, heretical and seditious
literature. Both institutions and individuals in eighteenth-century
France were generally engaged in the simultaneous pursuit of
multiple interests whose reconciliation called for much finesse.

The Second Estate grouped together a very heterogeneous nobility,
ranging from the Princes of the Blood through ancient warrior
families and the ennobled royal servants of past ages to the humbler
fry who had recently bought noble status or were in the process of
acquiring it through office. France differed from England in the fact
that all members of a family, and not merely eldest sons, were noble.
The French nobility also had much closer links with the army, most
men of distinction serving for a time, although many left after a few
years. These factors gave them a sharper sense of distinctiveness and
imparted a more martial character to the code of honour by which
they claimed to conduct themselves. This was something that struck
British travellers, who otherwise found a good deal in common
between the two societies. The specific privileges conferred by noble
status – exemption from some taxation and a near-monopoly of the
most coveted occupations – went with an aggressive assertion of
noble separateness; and it was difficult to win a lawsuit against a
great lord or to make him pay his debts.

In the army there was a gulf
between officers and men

Everyone else was part of the Third Estate, which ranged from the tramp to the millionaire banker or the country gentleman on the fringe of nobility. In France even more than in England, wealth was prized as a means to social advancement rather than as an end in itself. The successful bought land, office or securities in order to *vivre noblement* as a step on the road to nobility itself. A little lower in the social scale were the professional classes, mainly consisting of the various types of lawyers who proliferated in the innumerable courts of one kind and another. Like everyone else, the lawyers pursued their advancement in various directions at the same time and this could involve them in conflicts of interest. A man who still called himself de Robespierre, for example, joined the Arras bar at twenty-three, became a judge in the bishop's court a year later, and at thirty-one was a candidate for royal office in yet another court. Merchants, even affluent ones, enjoyed less esteem than members of the professions – though, if wealthy enough, they could help their daughters jump a rung in the social ladder by buying them noble husbands.

Middle-class prosperity was far removed from aristocratic elegance

Antique laws against usury, and relatively primitive systems of credit and insurance, made commerce a risky business; but many found that their luck held long enough for them to transfer their gains to safer investments with more social standing and to educate their sons for the professions.

The world of finance bridged the gap between nobles and Third Estate; the judges and consuls of the Bordeaux Bourse

Most of the urban population consisted of artisans, shopkeepers and servants. The artisans, unless they were the sons of master craftsmen, were finding it harder to become masters themselves, and journeymen were increasingly combining to demand higher wages, but they were a long way from behaving like a proletariat. Their guilds were centres of social life as well as professional organizations. Members were jealous of such evidence of their corporate status as the order of precedence of the various guilds in religious processions. Masters and journeymen shared many common interests, including the defence of their privileges against interlopers operating in the countryside, and townsmen united in opposition to food producers, since wage rates tended to be traditional whereas bread prices fluctuated a good deal from one harvest to another.

Conflicts of interest were no simpler in the village than anywhere else. Peasants might offer collective resistance to the tithe-owner or the manorial lord, but wealthy farmers, who bought the right to collect tithes or manorial dues and hoarded produce when scarcity was forcing up prices, shared some of the interests of the lay and clerical seigneurs whom they denounced, on other occasions, as rapacious landlords. The village tax-collector's responsibility for the payment of the tax assessed on the village as a whole was another divisive element. Tensions rose and fell with the harvest. A good crop meant food and work for all. A poor harvest increased the burden of the tithe, which was levied on gross production, not on profit, and put the poorer peasants at the mercy of those from whom they had to borrow grain, while the sight of full barns waiting for prices to rise, or loaded wagons leaving the hungry village, was a constant temptation to the kind of direct action that local opinion regarded as social justice rather than as theft.

Where France differed most strikingly from England was in its political life, in so far as it can be said to have had one. In theory the king's power was absolute and all authority was exercised in his name by the agents of his choice. The reality was somewhat different, but the absence of any constitution meant that the nation did not exist as a political unit – scarcely, indeed, as a political concept. There were no elections in the British sense, and, in a country only very imperfectly unified, interest focused on the defence of local privileges. Some of the more recently acquired provinces retained their local Estates, which bargained with the government about taxation in a kind of ritual ballet where the pretence of consultation softened the realities of power. The composition of the Estates of Artois shows how far these medieval survivals were from any genuine form of elective local government. The First Estate was restricted to a handful of the upper clergy and excluded the parish priests altogether. Most of the nobility were similarly kept out of the Second Estate. The membership of the Third Estate was even more peculiar. It consisted of the city councillors of Arras – whose mayor in 1789 also sat in the Second Estate since he was noble – together with representatives of certain towns. The latter had been elected in the past but when the Crown suppressed the right of election it had been bought back by the Estates. These 'representatives' of the Third Estate were therefore chosen by the body of which they were supposed to form part: in other words, by the clergy and nobility. Such arrangements, all sanctified by tradition, were too common to strike many people as odd.

The whole country was administered by royal officials known as Intendants. These agents of the royal bureaucracy were continually challenging the authority of the only bodies capable of resisting

them, the Church, the law courts and the provincial Estates. As always, however, official fictions were tempered by the facts of social life. The Intendant might be the king's man, with promotion to Minister as his ultimate professional ambition, but he was often a noble with his social sights set on placing a son in the local Parlement, perhaps, or advantageously marrying off a daughter. His personal aspirations had to be fitted into that complex network of family alliances and feuds which made the social life of the nobility such excellent training for a career in diplomacy.

Lavoisier, scientist and tax farmer, with his wife

Members of the *noblesse de robe* received by the king

The main challenge to royal power came from the dozen appeal courts or Parlements, bodies which Ministers had to cajole and intimidate in endless, inconclusive negotiations. The judges of the Parlements, most of them noble by birth and the rest ennobled *ex officio*, had bought their offices and could not be removed by the Crown. As the custodians of traditional law, they claimed the right to advise the king on the limits of his rightful authority. There was the usual wide, if fluctuating, gap between theory and practice. The king could enforce the registration of any law he wished and the Parlements could not prevent him. What they could do was to organize noisy public protests and resort to judicial strikes. The government then exiled them to uncomfortable towns without the social amenities to which they were accustomed. After a suitable interval negotiations were resumed, a face-saving compromise restored something very like the *status quo ante*, and both sides prepared for the next round. In this genteel trench warfare each side hoped for tiny concessions that could be enlarged into precedents, and the barrage of slogans about the sanctity of the royal prerogative or the inalienable rights of the subject obscured the very limited objectives of the combatants. To counterbalance the theoretical omnipotence of the king, the Parlements could generally rely on rivalry between his Ministers. The king needed the Parlements if the judicial system was not to break down and the most vociferous opponents of royal despotism were often aspiring to ministerial office themselves, so there was little danger of the conflict getting out of hand.

Opposite Louis XVI in his coronation robes

22

The fact that France had been ruled largely by negotiation since the death of Louis XIV in 1715 was due mainly to the character of his successors. Prerogative and patronage gave the king the means to make his authority effective if he had both the will and the ability to govern. In the last resort the only alternative to obedience was revolt, and no magnate could hope to challenge the powerful professional army. Louis XV and Louis XVI, however, neither ruled themselves nor delegated their power to a single chief Minister. This led to endless intrigue at Versailles and crippled the main source of innovation in a country bogged down in precedent. The king was not merely the head of state but also the centre of the Court. He had to live with his great nobles and he shared their ideas about what constituted fair play. Both his education and the company he kept made it unlikely that any Bourbon would emulate the absolutism of Frederick II of Prussia or Joseph II of Austria.

During the second half of the eighteenth century this whole interlocking system gradually began to move in new directions. Historians, with their penchant for regarding whatever happens as inevitable and for reading history backward in pursuit of causes, are inclined to see every new development as a step on the road to the Revolution. One has to be cautious about this. One school claims to have identified a 'seigneurial reaction', meaning a more business-like and systematic exploitation of manorial dues that exacerbated relations between peasants and their lords. Evidence for such activity certainly exists but it is not clear that it was increasing in the generation before 1789. To the extent that it was, indeed, it set most of the peasantry not against nobles, as such, but against the owners of manors and their agents. In France, unlike most of continental Europe, commoners could buy manors, although no one knows how many did. If there was indeed a seigneurial reaction there were probably a good many cases where the village communities found themselves in opposition to successful businessmen and their bailiffs – the very kind of people who were to welcome the Revolution. Nothing in eighteenth-century France was simple or clear-cut.

Another manifestation of the same trend is said to have been the growing social exclusiveness of the nobility. This was partly the obverse of the tendency for noble status to become obscured in a society whose increasing wealth allowed more men to live like nobles and buy army commissions for their sons. Here again, it is not difficult to find future revolutionaries such as Lazare Carnot and Madame Roland who had suffered from noble snobbery. But this did not stop Carnot from trying to invent a noble ancestry for himself and even a future terrorist, J.P. Marat, did the same thing. The recently ennobled also suffered from a growing tendency to emphasize length of lineage rather than nobility itself. It would be

difficult to prove that such social tensions were the cause of anything in particular, but the division between the successful and the disappointed did help to dictate choices when the Revolution actually happened.

A street market; one of the posters on the wall advertises the sale of a manor with its rights

Firmer conclusions can be drawn from the increasing assertiveness of the Parlements. This was not merely a matter of their opposing the royal government more frequently or with greater persistence. They also became more ambitious in their claim to be both the custodians of some shadowy medieval constitution and the defenders of the natural rights of all Frenchmen. Increasingly they used words like 'nation' instead of 'kingdom' and 'citizen' rather than 'subject', which encouraged the readers of their remonstrances to think in terms more appropriate to republican Rome than to royal France. Their tactics in their campaigns against what they came to denounce as 'ministerial despotism' were carefully studied in the legal circles that were to provide the Revolution with so many of its leaders. The Parlements themselves, each restricted to a particular part of the country and none of them in any way representative bodies, were

Necker, the saviour of the old order?

unsuitable vehicles for the exercise of constitutional power, as they were to discover to their cost, but in default of any genuinely political assemblies their opposition weakened royal absolutism in practice and helped to undermine it in theory.

There were other signs that the political climate was changing. Traditionally, a Minister was a man whom the king had honoured with his confidence. When that confidence was withdrawn the fallen Minister retired from Court, usually in temporary disgrace. During the War of American Independence Louis XVI found himself obliged to call on the services of Jacques Necker, a banker, a citizen of the republic of Geneva and a Protestant in a country where Protestants were still not officially tolerated. In 1781 Necker, whose religion excluded him from a seat on the Council of Finance, took the unusual step of resigning from office. He then published the *compte rendu au roi* that finance ministers submitted to the king on their dismissal. This scandalized official circles by making public the details of a budget that was still regarded as the private business of the king. Necker cultivated his reputation by means of his subsequent writings and his wife's salon, and when he returned from Geneva in 1787 he led what might almost be described as a Necker party. Antoine Barnave, the future revolutionary leader, said that he was the first French public figure to enjoy what could be called popularity; and Robespierre, in Arras, spoke of him as France's potential saviour. In August 1788 he was able to return to office more or less on his own terms.

Necker, the hero of 1788

One of Necker's successors at the Ministry of Finance, C.A. de Calonne, used modern methods in his attempt to activate the stagnant economy by generating business confidence. He reconstituted the defunct East India Company and employed a shady speculator, the abbé d'Espagnac, to try to force up the value of its shares. Calonne's rival in the Council of Ministers, the baron de Breteuil, hired another adventurer, the baron de Batz, and the Swiss refugee Etienne Clavière, to speculate in the opposite direction. The Batz-Clavière team in turn employed the comte de Mirabeau as one of their pamphleteers. Each of the men involved was to play an active part in the Revolution. Stock-exchange manipulation of this kind was something new in French politics and a far cry from the language of the official pronouncements of His Most Christian Majesty, Louis, by the Grace of God King of France and of Navarre.

As Calonne was well aware, the main concern of government in the years before the Revolution was the state of the royal finances. One can regard the growing insolvency either as the accidental product of fiscal mismanagement or as something inherent in the society of the *ancien régime*. France was probably a wealthier country than Great Britain, and its national debt was no greater than the British one. In each country the servicing of the debt accounted for about half the annual expenditure of the government. Where they differed was in the fact that the rate of interest in France was almost double that across the Channel. This implied a much higher level of taxation and less scope for any increase to deal with a specific emergency. When France took advantage of the American Revolution to avenge recent defeats at British hands – at the price of supporting rebels and republicans against their king – military and naval victories were purchased at the cost of turning a chronic deficit into an acute financial crisis. Necker bought personal popularity at the expense of future solvency when he financed the war, not by new taxation but by extravagant borrowing. After his retirement special war taxation was introduced for a limited period. When this expired at the end of 1786 the annual cost of servicing the debt had risen from 93 million livres at the accession of Louis XVI in 1774, to 318 million. The only alternative to bankruptcy was now a substantial increase in taxation, for which public opinion was not prepared. The government was therefore driven to the fiscal expedients that precipitated the Revolution. Put in these terms, the whole process seems to have been determined by defective fiscal policies. One could argue, however, that high interest rates and an inadequate return from taxation were inherent in a society where credit was endangered by primitive fiscal organization and the uncontrollable demands of an extravagant Court, in which clergy and nobles escaped much of the taxation that they could have afforded to pay.

Opposite Marie Antoinette at Versailles

However one sees the situation, the difficulty of increasing taxation drove governments to borrow. As increased deficits were covered by new loans the financial predicament eventually became so serious that the pursuit of solvency involved a fundamental reorganization of the regime.

In 1787 Calonne brought forward a radically new financial programme, designed to set the monarchy on its feet again. He proposed to tax all land, whether owned by clergy, nobles or commoners; he urged the Church to sell off its manorial rights in order to liquidate its debts; and when he encountered the predictable opposition of the first two Estates he appealed to public opinion with an attack on his opponents that he ordered to be read from the pulpits throughout the land. Calonne tried to have his proposals endorsed by an assembly of Notables, a nominated body chosen from the major office-holders of the country. The Notables resorted to parliamentary tactics, demanding the right to investigate expenditure before they discussed new taxation. They also used the more traditional methods of Court intrigue to have Calonne dismissed. His place was taken by Loménie de Brienne, the archbishop of Toulouse and the leader of the opposition in the Notables. Calonne's appeal to public opinion and the Notables' insistence that only the Estates General could authorize new taxation could almost be described as France's

Royalist France to the rescue of republican America: the departure of a volunteer

Opposite Marie Antoinette's Versailles; *above*, the Hamlet; *below*, the Belvedere

Calonne, Minister of Finance
between 1783 and 1787

introduction to what the English understood as politics. This was a
conflict that held the attention of educated opinion throughout the
country.

Brienne tried to implement the essential parts of Calonne's programme by more conciliatory means, but opposition hardened all
the time. The Paris Parlement created difficulties over the registration
of new fiscal legislation and the Assembly of the Clergy voted the
Crown only a fraction of the subsidy it expected. These corporate
bodies were eager to exploit this opportunity to reverse the bureaucratic centralization that had taken place during the previous
century. Some of their members thought merely in terms of restoring
the past. Others were inspired by the examples of England and the

American Revolution to work for the conversion of France into a genuine constitutional monarchy. Both sides shared a common short-term political objective which concealed widely differing views about the future shape of French society. The immediate aim was to force the king to call a meeting of the Estates General, a body representative of the three Orders, that had not met since 1614.

Brienne and Guillaume de Lamoignon, the Keeper of the Seals or Minister of Justice, eventually tired of trying to conciliate the opposition, and in May 1788 they resorted to a judicial *coup d'état*, which contemporaries described as a revolution. They drastically curtailed the powers of both Parlements and manorial courts, creating new royal courts that offered tempting careers to lawyers prepared to gamble on the permanence of the new institutions. The legal revolution and the new fiscal policies might have provided a basis for an agreement between the royal government and all those alienated by the privileged society of the *ancien régime*. In practice this did not happen and the lawyers of the Third Estate followed the Parlements in denouncing ministerial despotism. The opposition of the corporate

Calonne invites the Notables to choose which way they would like to be gobbled up by the fisc

33

A meeting of the Estates of Burgundy

France saved by Dauphiné, 1788

bodies was unexpectedly violent. Some of the provincial Estates declared for the Parlements. There were riots in one or two towns and signs that army officers would be reluctant to order their men to open fire on the supporters of their fellow-nobles. In Dauphiné an illegal gathering succeeded in reviving the old provincial Estates that had not met for over a century. Royal government seemed to be breaking down. Brienne agreed to convene the Estates General in 1789 and appealed to the public for suggestions about how its business should be conducted. This was taken to imply the end of political censorship, and the result was an extraordinary flood of pamphleteering, almost all of it hostile to the government. Many pamphlets kept to variations on the old theme of the iniquities of absolutism but, as the debate continued, there was a growing tendency for commoners to attack the Parlements and the nobility in general. This was probably what Brienne had intended but it did not do him any good.

He held out until August 1788 when the shortage of money that had thwarted him all along forced him to begin paying state debts in paper currency. It was significant of the changing times that this drove him out of office, although he still enjoyed the confidence of Louis and his Austrian queen, Marie Antoinette. Regretfully, they accepted Necker as his inevitable successor. Whereas Brienne, in traditional fashion, had behaved as the king's man once he had managed to force his way into ministerial office, Necker saw himself as a popular hero and a statesman in his own right, rather than as a royal servant. He called off the attack on the Parlements and made no attempt to manage the elections to the Estates General. France was now committed to major innovations of one kind or another, but the form they would take was still unpredictable and was to result partly from accident.

34

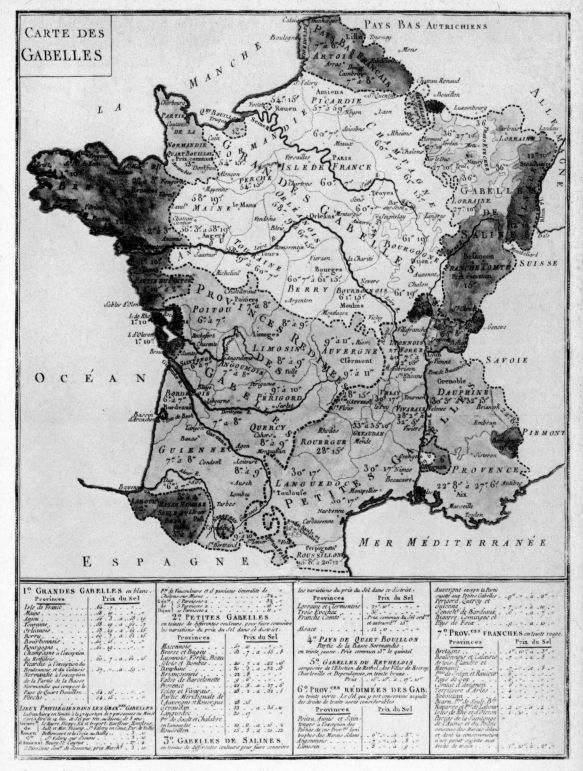

The variable incidence of the salt tax

CHAPTER TWO

The intellectual origins of the Revolution

The extent to which the French Revolution was the product of eighteenth-century political thought is one of those questions about which historians are never likely to agree. Different people assess the comparative importance of material and non-material factors in different ways. The present tendency is to emphasize economics at the expense of ideology. It has also to be remembered that the writers of the Enlightenment were not primarily concerned with political questions. They offered no common body of doctrine since they disagreed about the nature of the state and the objectives of political action. Their most influential works were published a whole generation before the outbreak of the Revolution. They were clearly not responsible for the revolutionary situation that developed in 1789 but they did dictate the terms in which educated people thought about society. When the Revolution happened, the men who emerged to lead it held quite well-developed views on what to do with the political power that had suddenly fallen into their hands. In this respect the French Revolution had more in common with the Russian than the English. In England there had been a greater tendency to improvise theories in the light of events.

The ideological inheritance of the Enlightenment offered three main intellectual systems. Although these were logically incompatible, practical men espoused parts of them all in a state of happy, if muddled, polygamy, borrowing such ideas as took their fancy or seemed to fit their experience. The revolutionary Assemblies themselves never made any final choice between the principles of Charles Louis de Secondat, baron de Montesquieu, and those of Jean Jacques Rousseau. There was nevertheless a certain inner logic within each of the systems that pointed toward a specific political option, and each is worth examining in isolation, provided we remember that no one tried to implement it *en bloc*. Even Robespierre said that there were some truths better left in Rousseau's writings than converted into legislation.

Montesquieu was for a time a member of the Parlement of Bordeaux. His *De l'Esprit des Lois*, published in 1748, combined a rationalization of *ancien régime* society, as seen from the viewpoint of the nobility, with a normative analysis in which the liberty of the

Opposite Mirabeau welcomed by the shades of Franklin, Montesquieu, Voltaire, Rousseau and Fénelon

An unflattering view of Montesquieu as a young man

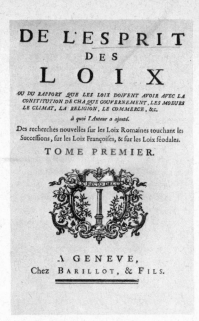

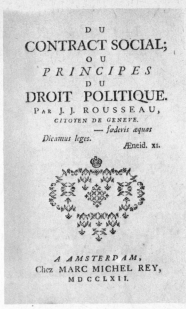

individual was presented as the cardinal objective of good government. Montesquieu, concentrating not so much on the location of power as on the way in which it was exercised, divided all government into three kinds. Despotism, based on fear, he quickly eliminated as the negation of acceptable government – an illustration of what happened when things went wrong. That left the republic and monarchy.

The republic, as he saw it, was an ideal society whose citizens subordinated themselves to the community as a whole. He implied that their collective self-interest was identical with morality, and the republic therefore represented the triumph of virtue. Since the required self-abnegation depended on qualities of the heart that were accessible to all and independent of formal education, the purest form of republic was a political democracy. Montesquieu was not sure whether such utopias had existed in ancient Greece, but quite certain that there was none in eighteenth-century Europe. The implications of building a society on such a basis interested him as an abstract thinker, but as a practical man he was much more attracted by the study of the actual functioning of the monarchies of which he had some personal experience.

Unlike a republic, a monarchy derived its dynamism from the fact that it allowed the most important subjects of the king to follow their natural inclination. This pointed not to wealth but to honour. Montesquieu freely admitted that the honour he had in mind was a bizarre quality, determined by social convention and quite unrelated to any system of ethical values. It was, however, the rule by which the nobility of Europe claimed to regulate its conduct. As such, it took

CAR. DE SECONDAT DE MONTESQUIEU.

N. le Mire del. et sc.

39

ENCYCLOPÉDIE,

OU

DICTIONNAIRE RAISONNÉ

DES SCIENCES,

DES ARTS ET DES MÉTIERS,

PAR UNE SOCIETÉ DE GENS DE LETTRES.

Mis en ordre & publié par M. *DIDEROT*, de l'Académie Royale des Sciences & des Belles-Lettres de Prusse; & quant à la PARTIE MATHÉMATIQUE, par M. *D'ALEMBERT*, de l'Académie Royale des Sciences de Paris, de celle de Prusse, & de la Société Royale de Londres.

Tantùm series juncturaque pollet,
Tantùm de medio sumptis accedit honoris! HORAT.

TOME PREMIER.

A PARIS,

Chez
BRIASSON, *rue Saint Jacques, à la Science.*
DAVID l'aîné, *rue Saint Jacques, à la Plume d'or.*
LE BRETON, Imprimeur ordinaire du Roy, *rue de la Harpe.*
DURAND, *rue Saint Jacques, à Saint Landry, & au Griffon.*

M. DCC. LI.
AVEC APPROBATION ET PRIVILEGE DU ROY.

Diderot's *L'Encyclopédie* as the epitome of the Enlightenment

precedence over both human and divine law. The Church might fulminate against duelling and the king declare it illegal, but there was general agreement that neither exile nor damnation should hold back the man whose honour had been called into question. Honour was a patrimony conferred by birth. Its essential characteristic was distinction, the possession of something to which others aspired. Its very nature therefore implied the existence of a hierarchical society. Titles granted by the king were only the recognition of the esteem in which a man was held by his peers, since honour was independent of

The award of the monarchy's highest order, the *cordon bleu*

both Church and State. It was, however, associated with service to the king – on one's own terms. The ruler enjoyed the benefit of cheap voluntary services, but only on conditions. Men would spend their lives as badly paid army officers for no more tangible reward than the ribbon of the Order of Saint Louis, but they reserved their right to retire at will and to seek service under foreign rulers if they chose. Whatever the Admiralty might think about things, the first preoccupation of the naval officer was with *l'honneur du pavillon* and not with the safety of the convoy under his escort.

Montesquieu recognized that, in a monarchy where people followed their own self-interest, any political body was a potential source of tyranny since it would identify the general interest with its own advantage. The preservation of individual liberty therefore depended on political machinery being skilfully contrived so as to balance the competing interests within a society, especially by means of the separation of legislative, executive and judicial authority. He thought he had identified such machinery in the British constitution, where the dangerous aspirations of king, lords and commons acted as checks upon each other, with an independent judiciary as the final protection for the subject against his interfering would-be masters. He believed that in France the main threat to the honour of the minority and the liberty of all came from the pretensions of bureaucratic absolutism. Louis XIV had dangerously weakened the intermediate bodies that had formerly shared in the exercise of power, with the result that France was moving toward despotism. Although a restoration of the previous balance was in the interests of all Frenchmen, only the predominantly noble corporate bodies, such as his old Parlement, had the means and independence of outlook necessary to exercise any effective restraint over the invasive royal government.

There is much more to *De l'Esprit des Lois* than that. It is, in fact, a somewhat neglected masterpiece of political and sociological theory. Its main relevance in the present context lies in the fact that it provided the provincial Estates and the Parlements with a splendidly respectable basis for their resistance to the royal government. They convinced themselves, and a good many other people for a time, that they were the last defenders of liberty against the exactions of arbitrary government. Far from being disloyal, they were preserving monarchy itself from the temptations of despotism. Fighting the good fight meant not only putting the king in his – rightful – place but preserving the hierarchical society of honour with all its social distinctions. Egalitarian radicalism, whether preached by social revolutionaries or rather timidly hinted at by Calonne and Brienne, could be sternly rebuked as the handmaiden of despotism. As cardinal de Beausset wrote to Cambacérès in 1789: 'When the corporations and orders have been destroyed or reduced to an empty name, there will be nothing left but democracy and a democracy of twenty-four million men leads straight to despotism.' So long as the Parlements were on the defensive it was not difficult to see them as the defenders of public liberty. It was only when victory seemed within their grasp, and the summons of the Estates General promised a return to the good old days, that their supporters realized the magistrates were as much committed to the social *status quo* as to political reform.

No one who reads the pamphlet literature of 1788–89 can fail to be impressed by the extent to which the writings of the Parlementaires

and their followers were dominated by Montesquieu. Quotation and paraphrase crop up everywhere. The Parlement of Nancy, to quote one example, accused Brienne of turning the monarchy into a despotism: 'The assimilation of social ranks, the abolition of their distinctive privileges, the extinction of intermediate bodies and subordinate authorities gradually undermines the foundations of monarchical government and prepares the way for arbitrary rule.' As the debate moved from the attack on 'ministerial despotism' to the question of privilege, Montesquieu's defence of the role of inter, mediate bodies found fewer supporters. A disgruntled conservative complained that 'people have now succeeded in bringing the masses to think that the word "privilege" is synonymous with injustice'.

Montesquieu's influence, however, outlived the Parlements. His view of the separation of powers and the need to divide authority if government was not to become tyrannical remained orthodox doctrine throughout the Revolution. Even his emphasis on the role of honour survived until 1792 although the concept was broadened, along English lines, to include the gentleman as well as the noble. He had not advocated a return to the past for its own sake and, despite many innovations that would have made him uneasy, he would probably have preferred the constitution of 1791 to the absolute monarchy under which he lived.

'The business going forward at present in the pamphlet shops of Paris is incredible' (Arthur Young)

Rousseau botanizing

Rousseau, whose main contribution to political theory, *Du Contrat Social*, appeared in 1762 and was reprinted a dozen times within a year, started with Montesquieu's assumption that republican regimes rested on the emotional identification of the citizens with the community to which they belonged. He, however, gloried in his status as a citizen of the republican city-state of Geneva. There was not much in common between Geneva and the idealized Athens or Sparta of the eighteenth century, and Rousseau's own relations with the city fathers were stormy enough. It was perhaps because he spent most of his life in France that this brilliant but unstable man was able to make a cult of his birthplace and to treat the republican form of government as the norm. His influence on his contemporaries was primarily emotional. He made them feel differently and his imaginative and incantatory prose, the antithesis of Montesquieu's cool classicism, worked on their hearts as much as on their minds. Barnave wrote of him, rather acidly, 'He had a great influence over the minds of the young and made madmen of people who would otherwise only have been fools. . . . He gave birth to that new style, a compound of enthusiasm, *vertu* and ardent sensuality, that has since dominated so much writing and rules so many heads.' Rousseau's best-selling novel, <u>La Nouvelle Héloïse</u>, spread his influence far

Rousseau, the enigmatic patron of the Revolution

A scene from Rousseau's opera, *Le Devin du Village*

beyond the people who read political theory. His political influence at the time rested less on his arguments about sovereignty, which have provided the material for so much subsequent controversy, than on the example of his tormented life and on those of his writings that had no explicit political content. The domestic arrangements of Julie, the heroine of *La Nouvelle Héloïse*, provided the prototype for the society that some of the more extreme revolutionaries were to advocate in 1794.

The essence of Rousseau's message for the men of his own age was that society was corrupted but capable of regeneration. He was primarily a moralist and what distinguished his converts was a crusading enthusiasm that looked like fanaticism to the unconverted. He rejected the salon doctrines of sophisticated self-interest and regarded the pursuit of material well-being as not merely frivolous but pernicious. Peasant communities – about which he knew very little – seemed to him the only part of society that had remained relatively uncorrupted by the false values of affluence. The emotional affinity between Rousseau and some present-day protest movements is obvious, though he was the reverse of an anarchist. Indeed, his old-fashioned puritanism implied extreme social discipline. He rejected both the society of honour and the pursuit of a higher standard of living as an end in itself, but his own social message was somewhat shadowy. He believed that a healthy community was incompatible with extremes of wealth and poverty, but he took the latter to be a

45

precondition of the former and said little about using political power in order to redistribute wealth.

In his specifically political writing he naturally advocated for the republican type of society the opposite of what Montesquieu had thought appropriate to a monarchy. Everything should be so organized as to enhance the effectiveness of the moral will of the community as a whole. Any society in which this will actually prevailed was a true republic, whatever the formal title of its rulers. The identification of this general will and its freedom of action depended on the destruction of those intermediate bodies, so dear to Montesquieu, which encouraged the assertion of sectional interests. Rousseau was a democrat, in the sense that he thought of all adult males as citizens – like his Revolutionary followers, he had no use for women in politics – but his was an authoritarian democracy. The moral infallibility of the general will, which reflected the true values of society as a whole, meant that opposition was not merely factious but wicked. When men, acting in the name of the general will, forced a dissident not merely to abstain from opposition but to agree that he had been wrong, they were merely forcing him to be free.

The future leaders of the Revolution were not concerned with the philosophical problems raised by this concept of the general will, although they were fond of using the expression itself. Rousseau had not invented the phrase, and it would be wrong to assume that anyone who used it afterward had necessarily borrowed it from him. Many, however, had; and in their hands it became a batteringram against the privileged corporate bodies and the sanctity of tradition. More important was Rousseau's conception of the state as the vehicle for the moral redemption of the citizen. It was this that gave a Promethean dimension to the political crisis engineered by the French nobility in 1789 and led enthusiasts all over the Western world to see the French Revolution as a turningpoint in the history of man. Robespierre was their spokesman when he said: 'The two opposing spirits that I have shown contending for dominion over nature [vertu and vice] are fighting it out in this great epoch of human history, to determine for ever the destinies of the world. France is the theatre of this terrible combat.' Few people are likely to agree with him now but unless, by an effort of the imagination, we can establish some sort of empathy with the men who felt themselves in the front ranks of this Homeric battle, we shall never understand very much about the Revolution.

At a less exalted level, Rousseau taught Frenchmen a new doctrine of the total sovereignty of the state. The abbé E. J. Sieyès wrote, in the most famous of all the pamphlets of 1789, Qu'estce que le Tiers État: 'The Nation exists before all things and is the origin of all. Its will is always legal, it is the law itself. . . . In whatever manner a nation

The abbé Sieyès, the man who slipped through the Revolution

wills, it suffices that it does will; all forms are valid and its will is always the supreme law.' This was a new idea which, for better and worse, was going to go a long way.

Rousseau's appeal to the emotions, his identification of morals and politics, his belief in the possible regeneration of man by secular means, and his total repudiation of contemporary society produced a far more explosive compound than he had ever intended. In the broadsides that opened the Revolution his influence is visible in both the radicalism of some political claims and the passionate language in which they were couched. 'When the rights of man are at stake,' to quote the *Cri d'un Français citoyen*, 'passion or enthusiasm is the essence of reason; only indifference is madness.' The 'social contract' was interpreted in ways that left no room at all for the autonomist aspirations of the nobility and only a nominal role for the king: 'The power of the prince is therefore never more than secondary and contingent since his moral authority derives from the general will. . . . The power of the Estates General is therefore superior to that of the monarch.'

During the early years of the Revolution the search for a compromise with the king and the nobility relegated the millenarian aspirations of the true Rousseauists to the political opposition. When his terminology was used, as in the Declaration of the Rights of Man of August 1789, which proclaimed that law was the expression of the general will, its more radical implications were ignored. After 1792, when the king had been dethroned and revolutionary France was at war with most of Europe (and with a substantial part of the French people as well), some of those in power made a conscious attempt to create the kind of society of which Rousseau had dreamed. Like Lenin after 1917, they tried to impose from above the kind of society and social values whose preexistence had been assumed by Rousseau and Marx. Unlike Marx, however, Rousseau had paid little attention to the economic basis of his regenerated society. His followers had few ideas on this subject beyond the revival of traditional controls in the interests of the consumer and the introduction of progressive taxation on a scale that would seem very modest today. This was partly because their Rousseauism was combined with elements of the third of the revolutionary ideologies: economic liberalism.

It is impossible to attach liberal ideas to the name of an individual. They emerged at about the same time in both England and France, drew on various sources and never formed a single unified doctrine. Initially they owed a good deal to a change in religious thinking that substituted a beneficent for a punitive deity. As early as 1733, in his *Essay on Man*, Pope had cheerfully dismissed the central problem of both Montesquieu and Rousseau, the resolution of the conflict between duty and selfinterest:

> *Thus God and Nature linked the general frame*
> *And bade Selflove and Social be the same.*

A generation later, the French Physiocrats based their economic theories on a similar conception of Providence. Agriculture was the only source of wealth: commerce and industry merely moved things around or put them together, whereas the annual miracle of the harvest allowed the farmer to reap a bushel when he had sown a peck. An age of growing religious indifference gradually transformed these theories in a way that was not merely secular but amoral. The

enrichment of society and its members came to be regarded as an end in itself, almost as the only end of politics. This could be regarded as a moral objective of a kind if one assumed, as most people did, that poverty was the main source of crime. Since Providence had ordained that the surest way to this goal was for each to seek his own advantage, all conflict, whether between classes or states, was the product of ignorance and prejudice. The role of government was restricted to scientific administration, and its main duty was to remove obstacles to the free development of individual initiative.

In some ways economic liberalism was the most radical of the three ideologies. Whereas Montesquieu and Rousseau had thought in terms of an economically static society, the liberals saw that, given free competition, the division of labour and the continual reinvestment of profits, the way was open to material progress on a scale never before imagined as possible. In the long run they were right and it is difficult for our own affluent society to criticize them without hypocrisy. In the short run, however, they had little to offer to the great majority. *Laisser-faire* in time of dearth meant the rejection of the idea, as Burke rather delicately put it, 'that it is within the competence of government, taken as government, or even of the rich, as rich, to supply to the poor those necessaries which it has pleased Divine Providence for a while to withhold from them'. They should, in other words, be allowed to starve. Even in good times, the law of supply and demand ensured that the reward of labour was the minimum necessary to keep the labourer working as an efficient tool

Glass-making, one of the few industries open to the nobility

Voltaire

Opposite Voltaire adopted by the Revolution

and allow him to reproduce his kind. This tendency to regard people merely as agents of production, whether investors of capital or 'hands', revolted both Necker and Robespierre.

The new attitude was equally uncongenial to many of the nobility, since it had no place for the non-material values that meant so much to them – for birth, family connections, even for honour itself. If it seemed to them the creed of upstarts, one must be wary of assuming that this made it the ideology of the bourgeoisie – whoever they were. It offered material rewards to the owners of capital, most of whom were landowners. Mining, quarrying and iron-smelting were considered, if not exactly as branches of agriculture, at least as activities ancillary to the exploitation of great estates. Whether one welcomed the new ideas and developed the economic potential of one's land, or whether one rejected them as socially subversive, was a matter of temperament and education rather than of class interest. They perhaps appealed most unequivocally to those with capital rather than status, but there were plenty of men with both who were prepared to welcome the initial stages of the Revolution as the means to both economic and social progress.

The political ideas of the economic liberals were ambivalent. Men like Voltaire, painfully conscious of the strength of conservative forces in French society and aware that any move toward representative government would strengthen the most backward-looking elements such as the Parlements, opted for enlightened absolutism. What mattered were the policies that governments pursued, and royal servants like Turgot, who was for a short time in charge of French finances after the accession of Louis XVI, or Calonne, seemed to offer the best prospect of scientific administration. It was not until 1789 that there was any real prospect of a government that would be both representative and forward-looking.

The fact that no sustained attempt was made to implement liberal policies before the Revolution has concealed some of the difficulties. Until the advent of railways there was no national market, and common sense restricted specialization and the division of labour if local famines were to be avoided. Practical administrators knew very well that, whatever the theorists said, it was simply not possible to enforce free trade in times of scarcity. With their old-fashioned ideas of a moral economy, peasants were not prepared to starve for liberalism; no government had the power to coerce all of them at once and they could rely on a certain amount of sympathy from traditionally minded squires and understanding parish priests.

By the time of the Revolution the new liberal orthodoxy was at least partially accepted by almost all educated opinion. In diluted form it could be combined with political ideas drawn from other sources. An English conservative like Burke would have endorsed the view

'An ass will always be an ass.'
Mesmerism as a refuge from
Reason

expressed by the radical revolutionary, Antoine de Saint-Just, in 1792: 'People are asking for a law about food supplies. Positive legislation on that subject is never wise.' One reason for the success of the revolutionaries in transforming France so quickly and with such lasting effect was this consensus of educated opinion. What they often did was translate into action schemes that former royal servants had kept in their pigeon-holes because the monarchy was too weak to overcome the resistance of the vested interests, which the new government took in its stride.

At the risk of repetition it is worth emphasizing again that contemporaries did not see the conflicts of the Revolution in terms of these abstract options. The most contradictory theories were thrown together as grist for their polemical mills. One pamphleteer, after making the Rousseauist claim that 'we are all born citizens; we are all *enfants de la patrie* before we become subjects of the king . . . the king is only the first subject of his kingdom', appealed for support

to both Montesquieu and Locke. What is clear is that men thought about politics in terms that had been defined for them by the Enlightenment. In the words of one of the many addresses to army officers: 'Beneficent philosophy has tempered your habits by enlightening your minds and taught you to know the value of being citizens.' There is no means of estimating the extent of the audience for the pamphlet literature of 1788–89 but it was certainly nation-wide and not confined to Paris. Pamphleteers in different parts of the country answered each other, and brochures like the *Letter of a gentleman of Dauphiné to a citizen of Toulouse* suggest the beginning of a national dialogue. The countryside may have been comparatively unaffected and much more concerned about the catastrophic harvest of 1788, but the entire legal world, polite society in the towns, the nobility and the clergy were all aware that they were living in a time of extraordinary intellectual ferment: and these were the men whose actions and reactions were to play the main part in the Revolution.

The king addresses the Notables

The general trend of the argument was overwhelmingly critical, first of the government and, by the autumn of 1788, of the aims of the Parlements and the nobility in general. After months of this kind of controversy, which became more and more embittered, it was clear that the Estates General would prove even more difficult to control than the Notables of 1787. A careful observer might have noticed that the object of attack was shifting from the iniquities of 'ministerial despotism' to the privileges and pretensions of the nobility. There was an opportunity here, if anyone was skilful enough to seize it, for an alliance between the Crown and the Third Estate.

The vocabulary and symbolism of the Revolution, as well as its political theories, were already fully developed before the Estates General met. Despotism was a 'hydra', the soldiery always 'unbridled' – unless of course they remembered that they were born citizens. Those who supported Brienne and Lamoignon had been damned, in one Parlement after another, as *infâmes* and *traîtres à la patrie*. Necker's restoration of the Parlements was celebrated with triumphal arches, obelisks and allegorical processions – all the paraphernalia of the later revolutionary fêtes. An enthusiast proposed as the emblem of Grenoble, capital of insurrectionary Dauphiné, a dolphin surmounted by a cap of liberty. Psychologically speaking, the Revolution had already begun.

Opposite A *cahier* from Paris

54

n° 22
39.e district

Cahier

De L'assemblée Partielle du Tiers État
de la Ville de Paris tenue dans l'Église
de Sorbonne le 21 et 22 avril 1789.

L'assemblée proteste avant toutes choses contre
le mode de convocation des assemblées de district,
en ce que les intérêts de la Capitale s'y trouvent
blessés par la destruction de la Commune, dont
tous ses habitans ont fait partie jusqu'à présent,
sans distinction d'ordres, et encore, en ce qu'on
n'a pas laissé le temps de pouvoir rédiger avec
soin les propositions particulières que chaque
assemblée de district auroit pu faire, pour
contribuer à la rédaction du Cahier Général:
en conséquence l'assemblée demande que pour
éviter de tels inconvéniens, il soit avisé dans
la prochaine tenue des États Généraux aux
moyens de fixer une forme de convocation
légale, et telle, qu'en réunissant tous les
Citoyens de cette grande Ville, elle procure à
chacun d'eux le double avantage de faire
connoître son voeu personnel, et de profiter
des lumières de tous: n'entendant néanmoins
ladite assemblée que la présente protestation
puisse retarder la tenue si désirée des États
Généraux, et priver le Royaume des fruits qu'il doit
se promettre de la réunion des connoissances
du zèle, et des Efforts des Représentans de toute
la nation.

L'assemblée se Bornera à présenter ici
l'apperçu Général des grands objets qui doivent

Suppression
des
Colombiers
Nuit du 4 au 5
Aout 1789

Dixmes
abolies

Justice Gratis

56

CHAPTER THREE

'Bliss was it in that dawn to be alive': 1789

The year 1789 saw the eruption of a political crisis that had been deliberately provoked by the Parlements, the provincial Estates and the upper clergy as a means of putting the monarchy in what they considered to be its place. Even before the end of 1788, however, they were beginning to wonder if they had not miscalculated. When Necker summoned a second meeting of the Notables in November, to discuss arrangements for the Estates General, those who attended were more apprehensive about the hostile pamphleteering of the Third Estate than aggressively disposed toward the Crown. They changed their policy and, whether from conviction or tactics, tried to alarm the king by insisting on the threat of the total subversion of all order. A memorandum signed by some of the Princes of the Blood declared that 'A revolution in the principles of government is in preparation. . . . The rights of the throne have been questioned; opinion is divided over the rights of the two Orders of the state [i.e. the clergy and nobility]; the rights of property will soon be challenged. . . . The proposal has already been made that to abolish feudal rights would [only] be to suppress a barbaric system of oppression.' The privileged Orders feared an alliance between the government and the Third Estate at their expense and suspected this was Necker's intention. De Bausset wrote in January 1789, 'I can only deplore the government's encouragement of the agitation of the Third Estate. . . . This policy was begun by the previous Minister [Brienne] . . . because of his resentment against the nobility, the judges and the clergy.'

It was sheer bad luck that this political crisis should have coincided with a catastrophic harvest. Crops had suffered in the previous July from a hailstorm of quite exceptional extent and severity. The British Embassy reported men being killed on the roads by hailstones sixteen inches round. 'It is certain that a Country at least thirty leagues in circumference [around Rambouillet] is entirely laid waste.' Farther to the north-east, the local Estates calculated that the damage in the province of Artois amounted to nearly two million livres (about £80,000). The inevitable result was that the price of bread, which always rose in the spring as stocks became exhausted, shot up to prohibitive heights. White bread in Hainault rose from $3\frac{1}{4}$ *sous* the pound in January to 6 *sous* in May, and remained at this level for

Opposite The suppression of seigneurial dues and tithes unites the three Orders over a month. In Artois the brown bread of the poor more than doubled in price between the end of 1788 and June 1789. Even in a normal year this would have meant serious trouble and stretched the forces of order to their limit. The English agronomist, Arthur Young, who was in France throughout the summer, wrote that he had often heard people say that 'the deficit would not have produced the revolution but in concurrence with the price of bread'.

Eighteenth-century administrators were well aware of the danger of anything that excited a credulous and largely illiterate rural population, deprived of any reliable sources of information. They knew that, in the most favourable circumstances, elections to the Estates General, for which all taxpayers were entitled to vote and every parish drew up its *cahier* of grievances, were only too likely to create trouble. The peasants were scarcely to be blamed if they thought that the whole unprecedented business meant the good king wanted to know of their complaints so that all wrongs could be swiftly righted. Such expectations kept them surprisingly orderly during the actual elections, but when their inevitable disappointment coincided with a dizzying increase in the price of their staple food the only question was what form disorder would take in the summer.

The hydra of taxation takes a beating

A BAS LES IMPIOTS

Le DEFECIT

Pub.d by S.W. Fores Nº 3 Piccadilly Novr 12.
I. Cruik.t
12 Nov. 1.

The elections to the Estates General, in March and April, were a wholly new political experience for the entire country. As new ambitions reinforced old animosities, local society was often torn apart by furious quarrels. On the whole the Third Estate was perhaps the least unruly of the three Orders. At Arras, and no doubt else-where, its main objective was to shake off the tutelage of the patrician oligarchy that claimed to dictate its choice of deputies, and this gave it a certain cohesion. The clergy were split almost everywhere by the revolt of the parish priests, each of whom had a vote, against the bishops, abbots and canons who had spoken in their name for so long. The British Ambassador, reporting that the bishop of Bayeux had been forced to resign the chair at Caen, continued, 'A similar spirit of opposition to the dignified Clergy prevails throughout the kingdom.' Things were no quieter in the Second Estate. The nobility of Lower Normandy refused to elect any office-holder or army officer; and the men who had formerly controlled the Estates of Artois, outvoted by the majority, walked out. The Breton nobility boycotted the Estates General altogether.

The deputies who gathered at Versailles at the beginning of May 1789 still bore the scars of these electoral battles. The First Estate,

Brienne makes off with the money while Necker assures the king he left the treasury full

Double representation for the Third Estate

with 291 deputies, was too bitterly divided between upper and lower clergy to act as a unified body; the parish priests were in the majority. The nobility, with 270 deputies, were split between courtiers and country squires; perhaps as many as a quarter were 'liberals' in the sense that they were prepared to surrender their separate status in return for citizenship in a regenerated France. The Third Estate had been granted double representation by Necker in the hope of conciliating public opinion, although this would not have much significance if the three Orders met and voted separately, with each having a veto over the other two. It consisted of 578 individuals, almost all of them unknown to each other and to the country at large, and without any party organization or political leadership. Most of them – lawyers from provincial towns, or substantial farmers – were not the kind of people normally regarded as 'radical'. They were men of property, very conscious of the gap that separated them from uneducated working men but resentful of the fact that nobles treated them as social inferiors and determined to seize this unique opportunity to reshape the country along different lines. To begin with, the men of a province tended to keep together and act as a group but, as the Assembly developed an identity of its own, political affinities took precedence over geography. At no time during the whole course of the Revolution, however, was there anything that resembled a disciplined modern party.

The marquis de Ferrières, who sat for the noblesse of Poitou, found the inaugural Mass of 4 May extraordinarily moving. Ferrières was not a grandiloquent man and his letters to his wife are endearingly fussy and practical. It meant a great deal when such a man burst out, in a private letter: 'I soon lost sight of the spectacle in front of me. . . . Love of my country, you made a deep impression on my heart. Until that moment I had not realized how powerful is the bond that links us all to the soil and to men who are our brothers. I swear, O France, object of my desire, where I was born and passed the happy days of my youth . . . never will I betray the confidence with which I was honoured when your interests were entrusted to my hands. Never shall anything alien to the good of all determine my judgment or my will.' It was an oath that was to see him safely through the Terror.

Private rhapsodies of this kind are likely to strike anyone who lives in an age of cynicism and denigration as less important than conflicts of material interest or the competition for office. That is not the fault of men like Ferrières. If we cannot respond to their feeling that all was about to be made new and better, we shall never understand 1789. Even the men involved could not recapture the atmosphere when those who survived looked back after years of bitterness, suspicion and disappointment.

The three Orders leave for Versailles, with the Third Estate driving and the clergy and nobility somewhat precariously balanced

The Estates General, awaited with so much eagerness, began as a resounding anti-climax. The government had granted double representation to the Third Estate without announcing whether voting was to be by head or, as in the past, by Order, with each Order having a veto over the other two. Everyone realized that if voting was by head, the minority of liberal nobles, the parish priests and most of the Third Estate would give the reformers a majority. In the hope of preventing this, the nobility quickly verified their credentials and declared themselves constituted as a separate Order.

For the opposite reason the Third Estate declared that all credentials must be jointly verified. Until this was done they refused to consider themselves as anything more than a gathering of people claiming election to a body that had not yet met. Attitudes hardened on both sides. The Third Estate acquired more confidence every day while the Court nobility made vigorous attempts to win over the squire-archy. Ferrières wrote naïvely to his wife on 5 June, 'The comte d'Artois [the king's brother] also treats me very well; he speaks to me every time we meet. . . . Would you ever have thought, my dear

The opening of the Estates General, 5 May 1789

63

friend, that your husband would be hobnobbing with Grandees!' Only a week later he was on his guard: 'There are a host of little intrigues in which I don't want to get involved.' Six weeks went by in inconclusive conferences. The price of bread was rising all the time.

Eventually the Third Estate broke the deadlock by taking the title of 'National Assembly', on 17 June, and refusing to recognize the mandate of any deputy whose credentials had not been verified in their presence. This forced the government, which had hitherto played a neutral role, to try to stop the situation getting out of hand. A royal session was announced, at which the king would make known his will. On 20 June the Third Estate, excluded from its usual meeting-place, which was being prepared for this royal session, and fearing a dissolution, held an emergency meeting in a tennis court and swore never to disband until France had a constitution. Two days later they were joined by half the clergy.

On 23 June the king addressed a joint session of the three Orders and for the first time produced a declaration of royal policy. On the constitutional issue he went farther than might have been expected. He accepted regular meetings of the Estates General, which was to have control over new taxation and the raising of loans and, up to a point, over government expenditure. He agreed to put a stop to arbitrary arrests by royal agents, to accept the principle of the freedom of the press, reorganize the law courts and introduce internal free trade. This was the end of Bourbon absolutism. On the other hand, Louis XVI went out of his way to guarantee to the nobility their separate identity and 'all rights and prerogatives, both material and honorific, attached to land, fief or person'. His declaration began with the blunt statement: 'The king wills that the ancient distinction between the three Orders of the state be preserved in its entirety as essentially bound up with the constitution of his kingdom.' He quashed the assumption of the title of National Assembly by the Third Estate and declared that the three Orders were to meet and vote separately on all issues affecting the particular rights of any one of them. He may not have realized it but he was endangering the monarchy in the defence, not of its own interests, but in those of the nobility.

One of the reasons for the hold of the Revolution over people's imaginations, both in France and elsewhere, was its abundance of dramatic incidents and memorable confrontations. The tennis court oath had already excited public enthusiasm. When the king had left the royal session and the Master of Ceremonies ordered the Third Estate to disperse, J. S. Bailly, who was in the chair, was reported to have replied, 'No one can give orders to the assembled nation.' The maverick noble, Mirabeau, added a touch of melodrama: 'We shall

Bailly, the first mayor of Paris

only leave our places at the point of the bayonet!' The abbé Sieyès reminded his colleagues that 'You are still today what you were the day before [i.e. the National Assembly]'. The king appeared to give way. On 27 June he even ordered the recalcitrant members of the clergy and nobility to join the majority.

The tennis court oath takes on a transcendental dimension

Convinced that the Revolution was now over, Arthur Young left Paris on 28 June to explore eastern France. Louis XVI, however, was merely playing for time, and the first orders had already gone out to concentrate troops on Paris. During the next fortnight rumours of these troop movements began to reach the Assembly, which complained to the King and was told to mind its own business. A force of nearly thirty thousand, many of them foreign units relatively immune to revolutionary propaganda, was expected to be available by mid-July. When most of the troops had arrived the king dismissed Necker and those ministers who sympathized with him. A trial of strength was now inevitable. The Assembly, with no force at its disposal, expected that the next moves would be its dissolution and the arrest of its leading members.

What followed took everyone by surprise. News of Necker's dismissal reached Paris on the morning of 12 June, a Sunday, which meant that anyone who wished to demonstrate had leisure to do so.

Desmoulins haranguing the
crowd in the Palais Royal

Urged on by excited orators, crowds began to gather and to call for
arms. X.X. Besenval, commanding the royal forces, ordered the
foreign regiment of Royal-Allemand to clear the Tuileries, and there
was a skirmish in which several civilians were wounded and one
reported killed. News of this 'massacre' brought the French Guards,
already succumbing to revolutionary propaganda, out of their bar-
racks to put their military training at the disposal of the resistance.
Besenval withdrew his troops to the outskirts of Paris. In the city
itself armed bands set fire to the customs posts where duties were
levied on incoming food, and began searching for hoarded grain,
sacking the convent of Saint-Lazare in the process.

The danger of anarchy was clear to everyone. Although the
occasion for the insurrection had been political, it seemed to be
taking the form of an immense hunger riot. In Versailles, the
Assembly was horrified by the rumour of pillage and arson but was
unable to take effective action. What turned the riots into a revolution
was the attitude of the Parisian electors, the men who had chosen the
city's representatives to the Estates General and who continued to
meet as a kind of political club. These men of education and com-

fortable means shared the reaction of the crowd to the dismissal of Necker, who was regarded as the main safeguard against both famine and bankruptcy. Instead of taking fright at the threat to life and property and asking for the protection of royal troops, they took over the city government and began raising their own militia, the National Guard, a two-edged weapon against both rioters and regular forces. The Guard was organized with remarkable speed:

Lambesc's troops charging the crowd in the Tuileries

The convent of Saint-Lazare sacked in the search for hoarded food

The city of Paris invests La Fayette with command of the National Guard

by the night of 13 July law-abiding citizens were reassured by the sound of armed patrols in the streets. Barnave commented, 'Most of the Paris militia is *bonne bourgeoise*, which makes it as sound for public order as it is formidable against tyranny.'

This new force, intended to reach a total of forty-eight thousand men, needed arms and munitions. On 14 July a crowd gathered outside the Invalides. As a result of a mistaken move by the governor and the refusal of the garrison of pensioners to fire on the demonstrators, the arsenal was ransacked without any fighting. It yielded thirty to forty thousand muskets and a dozen pieces of artillery but no powder. While this was happening the electors had begun negotiating with de Launay, governor of the medieval fortress of the Bastille at the opposite end of Paris, for access to his supplies of powder. De Launay, uncertain what to do, invited the deputies to luncheon, agreed not to open fire, but refused to allow the National Guard to occupy the Bastille. A crowd assembled outside and eventually broke into an outer courtyard. Someone opened fire and the result was a pitched battle, finally decided by the French Guards with four of the cannon from the Invalides. The assailants lost about a hundred men killed, the garrison one – though de Launay and half a dozen others were murdered after the fortress fell.

Cannon taken from the Invalides

Overleaf The cannon from the Invalides and the French Guards play a decisive part in the capture of the Bastille

The attack on the Bastille was the accidental product of its governor's vacillation. Its fall was proof of the resolution of the Parisians. The royal troops were promptly withdrawn from the neighbourhood and the threat to the city was over. This apparent proof that nothing could resist the forces of Revolution was seized on as something of exceptional importance. An English witness reported: 'The intelligence of this extraordinary event . . . produced an impression on the crowd really indescribable. A sudden burst of the most frantic joy instantaneously took place; every possible mode in which the most rapturous feelings of joy could be expressed were [*sic*] everywhere exhibited . . . such an instantaneous and unanimous emotion of extreme gladness as I should suppose was never before experienced by human beings.' The storming of the Bastille was the perfect symbol of the overthrow of the medieval past and of royal despotism – it had been the most famous state prison and had accommodated both Voltaire and Diderot at different times – by the heroism of the common man. The Assembly ordered the demolition of the fortress, and the contractor responsible did a thriving trade selling its stones as souvenirs. The extent to which the event caught

The end of the Bastille

the imagination of Europe is astonishing. The French Ambassador reported dancing in the streets of St Petersburg when the news arrived. Even the ranks of Tuscany could scarce forbear to cheer. The British Ambassador in Paris, who had little use for either radicals or Frenchmen, conceded that 'The greatest Revolution that we know anything of has been effected with, comparatively speaking, if the magnitude of the event is considered, the loss of very few lives.' The tale lost nothing in re-telling, as in Blake's poem, *The French Revolution*:

> *In its terrible towers the Governor stood, in dark fogs*
>   *list'ning the horror*
> *A thousand his soldiers,[1] old veterans of France,*
>   *breathing red clouds of fire and dominion . . .*

No one seemed to have many tears for de Launay and the handful of other victims of mob violence. Even the humane Ferrières took it all in his stride. 'I should never have thought that a good and easy-going people would have perpetrated such excesses but divine justice often makes use of human hands.'

Dancing on the ruins of the Bastille

---

[1] Actually, about 110; and the 'veterans' were, in fact, pensioners.

The duc d'Orléans as a
National Guard

Counter-revolutionary views
get rough treatment

Although it was the bloody and dramatic events in Paris that caught everyone's imagination, of more practical importance was the fact that similar municipal revolutions occurred in most of the towns of France. The objectives were everywhere similar – the overthrow of patrician oligarchies, the raising of National Guards and the occupation of military strongpoints – though not all were obtained in every case. In the course of a few days control of the country and its communications escaped from the hands of the royal government. It was this that led the Minister of War to reply to suggestions that the king should escape from Versailles, 'We can get to Metz, but what are we going to do when we have got there?' Louis resigned himself to the inevitable and recalled Necker. The comte d'Artois and his associates left the country. There could be no question now of stopping the Revolution by force – unless the force came from abroad.

A crisis of this magnitude sent shock-waves of rumour over the country. To judge from his style, Ferrières was still not quite himself

The *Grande Peur*: the château is burned but its owner is allowed to leave unmolested

when he wrote home: 'The fall of the Bastille certainly saved us. It is certain that the nights of Tuesday the 14th and Wednesday the 15th would probably have been our last day'. If educated deputies could think that the Court intended to have them murdered it is not surprising that peasants believed the queen and Artois were plotting to blow up the Assembly.

In the countryside tension was already rising, in any case, with the approach of the harvest when the ripening crops were most vulnerable to natural calamities and to arson. As reports of an aristocratic plot swept through the hungry villages there were widespread agrarian revolts. These involved surprisingly little loss of life. The peasants were generally content with the destruction of manorial records, though they sometimes burned down châteaux as well. These

Opposite Taking precautions: a seigneur fraternizes with his peasants

revolts were almost immediately followed by the strange phenomenon known to historians as the *Grande Peur*. This was, in fact, a number of separate alarms which spread quickly across most of the country. The characteristic of the *Peur* was the conviction that brigands had actually arrived and were burning the crops, poisoning wells and massacring the local population. Age-old memories helped to identify them: English, Spaniards, Piedmontese – though it is hard to imagine what folk-memories could have been responsible for the Poles, who were said to have landed on the Atlantic coast! The local reaction was not fear but anger. Villages stood to arms and sent flying squads to each other's support. Almost everyone believed the stories at first. Arthur Young repeated them on 27 July though he ridiculed them five days later. When the brigands failed to materialize, the mobilized peasants sometimes took advantage of the opportunity to sack the château of an unpopular seigneur. When the crisis subsided people not unnaturally felt – like Englishmen at the time of the non-existent German landing in September 1940 – that there must have been something behind it. There was a tendency to attribute the whole business to some aristocratic plot and the country-side emerged from its *peurs* in an angry and suspicious mood.

The enemies of the common people included lawyers (*bottom*) as well as the seigneurs' gamekeepers

The Assembly, after it had been saved by the municipal revolt, had begun work on the new constitution when news of these un-welcome events broke in on its euphoric debates. As information about genuine riots and château-burning coincided with the reports of the ubiquitous brigands, it was impossible for anyone to dis-tinguish truth from rumour and the deputies got the impression that the whole country was going up in flames. The Revolution in the towns had gone entirely in their favour, transferring power to their supporters, while the National Guard units that were being formed all over the country reassured those afraid of a threat to property. They had nothing to gain from violence in the countryside since many were themselves landowners or legal agents of landowners. On the other hand, to invite the king to restore order by force would antagonize the mass of the population and once the army had started to fire on civilians it might not stop at peasants. To add to the difficulty of the choice between repression and appeasement, many deputies felt that to abolish manorial dues would be to infringe the sacred rights of property.

They found a way out of their dilemma on 4 August. Tactics were decided in the club founded by the Breton deputies, which became known as the Jacobin club since it met in premises rented from the Dominicans, whose nickname was 'Jacobins'. This club had become the political headquarters for all the radical deputies. At the evening session of the Assembly, when many of the nobility were absent, two liberal nobles suggested that their Order should freely

renounce some of its manorial rights, thus evading the question of expropriation. Their initiative set off an astonishing spectacle that had probably not been planned by the Jacobins. One deputy after another from the first two Orders stood up to renounce his own – or occasionally someone else's – privileges. There were so many that they had to queue. In the space of a few hours, personal obligations to manorial lords were abolished without compensation and perpetual rents made redeemable for cash; hunting rights were suppressed; manorial justice followed, together with tithes and all manner of fiscal privileges. The venality of offices went the same way, as did the privileges and exemptions of towns and provinces. Justice was henceforth to be free, all occupations were thrown open to all competitors and the clergy offered to surrender all benefices held in plurality above a total of about £150.

This was the most ambitious day's work ever performed by any parliament. It was the opposition's amendment to the king's speech of 23 June and it transformed the entire political situation. Instead of confining itself to drafting a constitution, which should not have taken more than a month or two, the Assembly was now committed to the transformation of virtually all the country's institutions.

Before and after: the underdog
now holds the balance

The indulgent confessor: the Third Estate in a magnanimous role

Implicit in the 'renunciations' of 4 August was the creation of a new system of local government, the reorganization of all the law courts, a new fiscal structure, drastic changes in a Church that was deprived of about half its income and the transformation of the armed forces, hitherto the preserve of the nobility. The Assembly worked with astonishing speed, but this was a programme for years rather than months. When it was completed France would emerge as a new country. The deputies exaggerated when they claimed to have destroyed the feudal system in its entirety, but they had certainly pronounced the death of the *ancien régime*.

Modern historians have tended to adopt a curiously niggling approach to these memorable events. They have concentrated on the question of manorial dues and on attempts made during the drafting debates of the following week to whittle down some of the original concessions. There is something in these criticisms, and the text that emerged on 11 August was somewhat less generous than the original draft. The deputies adopted a conservative point of view when they came to decide which manorial obligations were to be preserved as property; and the conditions on which the others could be redeemed were beyond the means of the great majority of peasants, who were not relieved of their burden until 1792 and 1793. Although the peasantry as a whole gained from the abolition of hunting rights and the manorial monopoly of corn-mill, oven and wine-press, tenant farmers discovered that their leases were raised as landlords added the equivalent of the suppressed tithe. The legislation of 4 August certainly amounted to much less than a social revolution where property was concerned but it did create a new kind of society.

Some contemporaries had their reservations. 'How like our Frenchmen,' said Mirabeau, 'they spend a whole month quarrelling over syllables [about the Declaration of the Rights of Man] and within a night they overthrow the whole traditional order of the monarchy.' His was not a typical reaction. The constitutional fiction that what had happened was the generous renunciation of privileges by those who benefited from them, did generate a remark-able feeling of fraternity. 'What a nation, what glory, what an honour to be a Frenchman!' wrote François Duquesnoy, a deputy of the Third Estate. Ferrières, who had a good deal to lose, called the session 'the most memorable ever held in any country. It is typical of the noble enthusiasm of the Frenchman. It shows the whole universe his generosity and the sacrifices of which he is capable when honour, love of the public good and heroic patriotism are in command.' Even the king's sister, a stickler for the rights of the monarchy, told a friend: 'The nobility, with an enthusiasm worthy of their French hearts, have renounced all their feudal rights and hunting rights . . . it was a competition to see who could sacrifice the most; they were all magnetized.' This was the almost universal mood at the time. Its gradual erosion by hatred and suspicion is one of the great tragedies of the Revolution. Bailly, who was mayor of Paris at the time, was well aware of this. When he came to write his memoirs two or three years later he commented sadly on the famous night, *Beaux moments, qu'êtes-vous devenus?* Even Ferrières, in later years, thought that 'a feeling of hatred, the blind passion for vengeance and not the desire for good, seemed to fire people's minds'.

Louis XVI did not share in the general enthusiasm. It was too late for him to think of taking forcible action against the Assembly so he resorted to a policy of passive non-co-operation and failed to promulgate the decrees of 4 August and the Declaration of the Rights of Man. This immediately raised the question of whether the Assembly was a sovereign constituent body or whether all its proposals required the royal assent – which most of them were unlikely to get. The deputies, convinced that there was no practical

Opposite Mirabeau

alternative to the monarchy, were reluctant to apply more than verbal constraint. Their inhibitions were not shared by radicals in Paris, and pressure began to build up in the capital for a march on Versailles to intimidate the king. The summoning of the Flanders Regiment to reinforce the royal bodyguard at the palace, and the subsequent 'orgy' when its officers, somewhat the worse for drink, joined the ladies of the Court in an anti-revolutionary demonstration, provided the journalists and street orators with a field day. As usual in 1789 and throughout most of the Revolution, political issues became entangled with concern about food supplies. Bread was scarce in Paris. The harvest had been good, but the recent troubles had deterred growers from sending their grain to market and the fine summer was interfering with both wind- and water-mills. Rumours spread that there was plenty of bread to be had at Versailles. On 5 October a crowd of several thousand women seized such arms as they could from the town hall and set off on the long march to the royal palace. Later in the day the National Guard, perhaps twenty thousand strong, forced their commander, the Marquis de La Fayette, to take the same road. They at least were not primarily concerned with bread.

The king realized the political implications of what was happening and promptly gave the royal assent to the various acts of the Assembly. The women were more or less pacified with promises and the National Guard was entrusted with the maintenance of order outside the château. Early on the morning of 6 October some of the Parisians who had found nowhere to sleep broke into the château and

The provocative royalism of the Flanders Regiment

murdered one or two of the royal bodyguards. They forced their way into the queen's apartments, from which Marie Antoinette had barely time to escape. With the whole palace in an uproar the crowd invaded the courtyard and insisted on the royal family moving to Paris, where they would be hostages of the Revolution.

Henceforth the king and queen were committed to some form of counter-revolution, although they suspected Artois and his attempts to organize foreign intervention. An important minority within the Assembly, convinced that things had gone too far, hoped to check the Revolution and come to some compromise with the king. The British Embassy had recovered its sense of perspective after the heady events of July. A dispatch, reporting the removal of the royal family to Paris, continued: 'The blind and headlong will of the Populace directs all and all submit with fear and trembling to their Government as the dangerous maxims that all men are equal and that numbers can overcome a few, are in the mouths of every vagabond at present. Nothing is now left to the superior class of people but submission and the well proportioned exercise of that Policy, reason and education which may in time give them again the superiority over the Multitude.' There were a good many people, not all of them in France, who were far from being distressed by the dangerous maxim that all men are equal, but the *beaux moments* were already beginning to recede.

Bringing back the baker: the royal family conducted to Paris

British cartoonists were not impressed by 'democrats'

CHAPTER FOUR

New wine and old bottles: October 1789–September 1791

The Estates General, or Constituent Assembly as it now called itself, remained in session until September 1791. The fact that roughly half its members were nobles or clergy ensured that the divisions of the country would be reflected within its parliament. Debates, often noisy and acrimonious, were also very long-winded, since deputies trained in the academies and lacking political experience were inclined to bombard each other with prepared speeches. They were at their best in the committees whose prodigious activity reshaped the whole structure of the country. Until the King's flight from Paris in June 1791 they were not distracted by serious agitation in the capital and conditions in most towns were relatively calm. The diary of the American Ambassador, Gouverneur Morris, shows that the futilities of the less intelligent salons continued as before, with politics providing polite society with new topics of conversation and opportunities for intrigue. Disorder was more serious in the countryside, where good harvests did not prevent outbreaks of violence and château-burning. Things might have been – and were to become – much worse, but there was a general feeling of insecurity. The reluctance of the king to accept the measures he could no longer prevent, the emigration of some of the nobility who left the country (not from fear, but in the hope of returning at the head of an army of intervention), and the existence of counter-revolutionary plots at home, which were real enough, if not quite so hair-raising as good *patriotes* were inclined to believe: all these things meant that the euphoria of 1789 gradually gave way to suspicion, hatred and fear.

This process was considerably accelerated by the emergence of a vitriolic and scurrilous press. Scores of newspapers, most of them ephemeral productions, libelled politicians of every colour with outrageous impunity. The Grub Street hacks had come into their own and were using the Revolution to avenge themselves for the *ancien régime*'s disregard of what they considered to be their talents. The suspicion that some of them had not outgrown their old habit of writing whatever their secret paymasters dictated, discredited some of their more lurid 'revelations'. There were quite a few responsible editors and reputable newspapers as well, and it is impossible to assess the extent of the audience for the peddlers of plots or their responsibility for the deepening social animosities. Whatever the

Opposite France united: the Fête de la Fédération of 14 July 1790

cause, the social temper was certainly becoming increasingly sour and this was not confined to Paris.

The Assembly would never have had the self-confidence to set about the transformation of French institutions if it had not been able to rely on the ideological legacy of the Enlightenment. Most of the deputies believed that tradition did not matter and that the slow accretions of precedent and *ad hoc* improvisations could be replaced by a state constructed in accordance with principle. Their aim was to reorganize the country on lines that were rational and uniform, to make every kind of public office elective, to destroy the administrative centralization of the monarchy and to infuse all their work with the humanitarian ideas of the *philosophes*. The Declaration of the Rights of Man, voted in August 1789, was intended as a statement of the principles by which all future governments – not merely French ones – might be judged. It asserted the principles of popular sovereignty, representative government and the rule of law. Freedom of opinion, 'even' of religious opinion, liberty of the press and the sanctity of property, were familiar enough in England, but not in continental Europe. Much of the Declaration rested on a surprisingly wide basis of agreement in France; the King himself had accepted a good many of its principles in his speech to the Séance Royale on 23 June. The explosive potential of Article I ('Men are born and remain free and equal in their rights. Social distinctions can only be founded on public utility') would depend on the way in which it was interpreted. The Declaration has been criticized for its negative

Opposite The Declaration of the Rights of Man

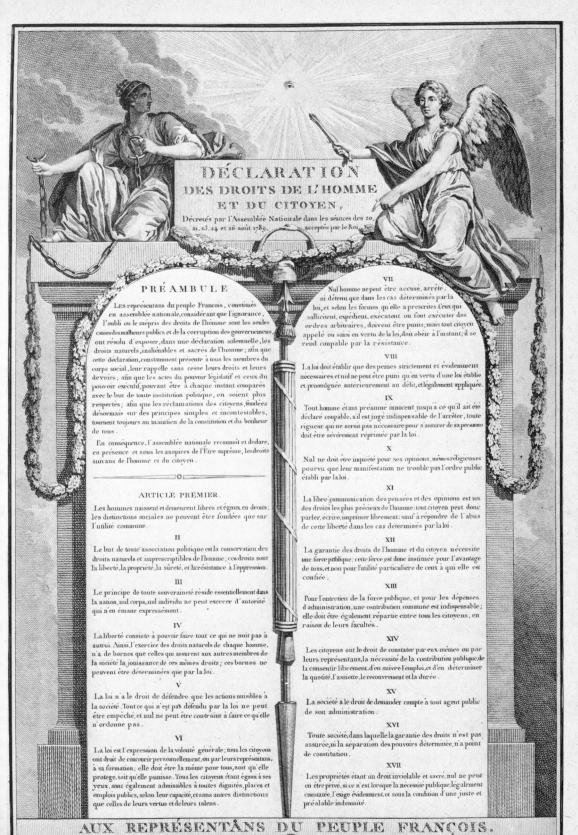

DÉCLARATION
DES DROITS DE L'HOMME
ET DU CITOYEN,
Décretés par l'Assemblée Nationale dans les séances des 20,
21, 23, 24, et 26 août 1789, acceptés par le Roi.

PRÉAMBULE

Les représentans du peuple François, constitués
en assemblée nationale, considérant que l'ignorance,
l'oubli ou le mépris des droits de l'homme sont les seules
causes des malheurs publics et de la corruption des gouvernemens,
ont résolu d'exposer, dans une déclaration solemnelle, les
droits naturels, inaliénables et sacrés de l'homme ; afin que
cette déclaration, constamment présente à tous les membres du
corps social, leur rappelle sans cesse leurs droits et leurs
devoirs ; afin que les actes du pouvoir législatif et ceux du
pouvoir exécutif, pouvant être à chaque instant comparés
avec le but de toute institution politique, en soient plus
respectés ; afin que les réclamations des citoyens, fondées
désormais sur des principes simples et incontestables,
tournent toujours au maintien de la constitution et du bonheur
de tous.

En conséquence, l'assemblée nationale reconnoît et declare,
en présence et sous les auspices de l'Être suprême, les droits
suivans de l'homme et du citoyen.

ARTICLE PREMIER.

Les hommes naissent et demeurent libres et égaux en droits ;
les distinctions sociales ne peuvent être fondées que sur
l'utilité commune.

II

Le but de toute association politique est la conservation des
droits naturels et imprescriptibles de l'homme ; ces droits sont
la liberté, la propriété, la sûreté, et la résistance à l'oppression.

III

Le principe de toute souveraineté réside essentiellement dans
la nation, nul corps, nul individu ne peut exercer d'autorité
qui n'en émane expressément.

IV

La liberté consiste à pouvoir faire tout ce qui ne nuit pas à
autrui. Ainsi, l'exercice des droits naturels de chaque homme,
n'a de bornes que celles qui assurent aux autres membres de
la société la jouissance de ces mêmes droits ; ces bornes ne
peuvent être déterminées que par la loi.

V

La loi n'a le droit de défendre que les actions nuisibles à
la société. Tout ce qui n'est pas défendu par la loi ne peut
être empêché, et nul ne peut être contraint à faire ce qu'elle
n'ordonne pas.

VI

La loi est l'expression de la volonté générale ; tous les citoyens
ont droit de concourir personnellement, ou par leurs représentans,
à sa formation ; elle doit être la même pour tous, soit qu'elle
protege, soit qu'elle punisse. Tous les citoyens étant égaux à ses
yeux, sont également admissibles à toutes dignités, places et
emplois publics, selon leur capacité, et sans autres distinctions
que celles de leurs vertus et de leurs talens.

VII

Nul homme ne peut être accusé, arrêté,
ni détenu que dans les cas déterminés par la
loi, et selon les formes qu'elle a prescrites. Ceux qui
sollicitent, expédient, exécutent ou font exécuter des
ordres arbitraires, doivent être punis ; mais tout citoyen
appelé ou saisi en vertu de la loi, doit obéir à l'instant ; il se
rend coupable par la résistance.

VIII

La loi doit établir que des peines strictement et évidemment
nécessaires, et nul ne peut être puni qu'en vertu d'une loi établie
et promulguée antérieurement au délit, et légalement appliquée.

IX

Tout homme étant présumé innocent jusqu'à ce qu'il ait été
déclaré coupable, s'il est jugé indispensable de l'arrêter, toute
rigueur qui ne seroit pas nécessaire pour s'assurer de sa personne
doit être sévérement réprimée par la loi.

X

Nul ne doit être inquiété pour ses opinions, mêmes religieuses,
pourvu que leur manifestation ne trouble pas l'ordre public
établi par la loi.

XI

La libre communication des pensées et des opinions est un
des droits les plus précieux de l'homme : tout citoyen peut donc
parler, écrire, imprimer librement ; sauf à répondre de l'abus
de cette liberté dans les cas déterminés par la loi.

XII

La garantie des droits de l'homme et du citoyen nécessite
une force publique : cette force est donc instituée pour l'avantage
de tous, et non pour l'utilité particulière de ceux à qui elle est
confiée.

XIII

Pour l'entretien de la force publique, et pour les dépenses
d'administration, une contribution commune est indispensable ;
elle doit être également répartie entre tous les citoyens, en
raison de leurs facultés.

XIV

Les citoyens ont le droit de constater par eux-mêmes ou par
leurs représentans, la nécessité de la contribution publique, de
la consentir librement, d'en suivre l'emploi, et d'en déterminer
la quotité, l'assiette, le recouvrement et la durée.

XV

La société a le droit de demander compte à tout agent public
de son administration.

XVI

Toute société, dans laquelle la garantie des droits n'est pas
assurée, ni la séparation des pouvoirs déterminée, n'a point
de constitution.

XVII

Les propriétés étant un droit inviolable et sacré, nul ne peut
en être privé, si ce n'est lorsque la nécessité publique, légalement
constatée, l'exige évidemment, et sous la condition d'une juste et
préalable indemnité.

AUX REPRÉSENTÅNS DU PEUPLE FRANÇOIS.

attitude to the state, and it was certainly more concerned with individual freedom *from* interference rather than with the right *to* employment or education. It would be unreasonable to expect any more at the time and even a judge as critical as Robespierre maintained to the end of his life that the Declaration needed only minor amendments. As he saw it, the problem was not so much to improve it as to implement it.

The 'renunciations' of 4 August had involved scrapping most of the administrative structure of the country. Before 1789 this was a civil servant's nightmare, with its 35 provinces, 33 Intendants, 13 Parlements, 38 military districts, 142 dioceses and innumerable local tolls and internal customs frontiers that kept thousands employed either in smuggling or its prevention. The old provinces were now divided into what are still, in most cases, the present departments. The department itself was split into several districts, and the districts into communes which varied in size from a hamlet to Paris itself. Each department, which was administered by an elected council, contained a single criminal court, each district a civil one. The previous labyrinth of overlapping courts and disputed jurisdictions had allowed wealthy or obstinate litigants to go on appealing almost indefinitely, so that pending lawsuits formed an important part of the assets and liabilities of most estates. Henceforth, civil cases had to start before a *bureau de conciliation* which tried to deter the parties from going to law at all. If they persisted, only one appeal was possible, from the initial verdict of the district court to a second court in a different district. Criminal cases were referred by justices of the peace to the departmental courts, from which there was no appeal. A central appeal court in Paris could order retrials only on procedural grounds. All criminal cases were to be tried by juries – in itself a revolutionary innovation in French justice. All judges were to be elected.

The instrument of revolutionary justice

In the *ancien régime* the law itself had been as confused and complicated as the courts that administered it. In the short run the spate of revolutionary legislation may have added to the difficulties; and the codification of French law had to wait for Napoleon. Some at least of the prevailing barbarities were abolished. Branding disappeared, and breaking on the wheel was replaced by a decapitating machine whose swift and relatively painless operations were so warmly commended by one of the deputies, Dr Guillotin, that it was named after him. At the time this looked like a compliment. Two deputies, Maximilien Robespierre and Adrien Duport, made a strenuous effort to have the death penalty abolished altogether. Although they failed, it was reserved for only a handful of offences, in marked contrast to the situation in Great Britain. Regular criminals, who knew how far they could go under the old system,

The Third Estate takes up the mantle of the nobility

disliked the new courts and their unpredictable juries, but the legal profession accepted the changes with surprisingly little difficulty – they were, after all, proposed by distinguished lawyers – and people in general had much to gain from them.

The Assembly's concern for both equality of opportunity and humanitarianism was illustrated by its treatment of the profession of arms. The purchase of commissions was abolished in the army – there was no equivalent in the navy – and all ranks were thrown open to commoners. A quarter of the sub-lieutenants were to be drawn from the ranks, the remainder being chosen by competitive examination. The conscripted militia, bitterly hated by the peasants on whom the entire burden fell, was abolished. The regular army was manned by voluntary enlistment and the nation-wide National Guard made the militia unnecessary. The navy continued to demand the compulsory service, on a rota basis, of the seafaring population, but the officials responsible for mobilizing the seamen were henceforth to be elected. New penal codes abolished the more ferocious punishments in both services, and servicemen were to be tried by military juries.

Since the Assembly was meticulous in discharging the obligations incurred by the royal government, the payment of compensation for

The funeral of the clergy

A revolutionary curé takes the oath to the Civil Constitution of the Clergy

the myriad of suppressed venal offices greatly increased the National Debt. A sum of the order of £25–30 million had to be found for this purpose alone. The revolutionaries also put an end to the monarchy's practice of making contractors wait two or three years for payment, which had raised prices and complicated budgeting. This again involved heavy expenditure while the arrears were being paid off: in 1789 the navy's debts amounted to more than a year's normal expenditure. There was no possibility of finding funds on this scale out of revenue, even allowing for a modest increase in the yield of taxation when fiscal privileges were abolished. What was needed was a massive influx of capital and this could only come from the sale of the Church's extensive properties in both town and country.

The deputies, while not hostile to religion as such, had little sympathy for the Catholic Church when considered as one of the three Estates of the realm. On this, at least, both nobles and commoners were agreed and the clergy themselves, for both worldly and unworldly reasons, failed to put up a united defence. It was Talleyrand, their former Agent Général, who first proposed the alienation of some of their property. In February 1790 perpetual monastic vows were abolished and those who wished to remain in monastic orders were regrouped so that many of their almost empty buildings could be put on the market. Deprived of both property and tithes, the clergy were dependent on what the state chose to pay them. This would have to be a good deal less than they had paid themselves in the past, if much was to be saved to pay off the state's debts. The

Civil Constitution of the Clergy, which the Assembly voted in July 1790, reflected both the need for economy and the determination of the deputies to reorganize the Church in accordance with the principles that they applied in secular matters. The number of dioceses in a department was reduced to one, parishes were redrawn in accordance with present population and most of the non-parochial offices were suppressed. All priests, including the bishops, were to be elected by the population at large, although the choice of the electorate required ratification by the appropriate ecclesiastical body. The deputies regarded this as part of their general programme, and their intention was to create a Church better equipped for the discharge of its spiritual duties. The clergy, however, were not merely an Order of *ancien-régime* society but also part of an international church. Claiming that the Assembly was trespassing on matters spiritual, the leading clergymen in the Assembly insisted that the Civil Constitution required the assent of either an assembly of the French clergy or of the Pope. The Assembly refused them the right to convene the former and the Pope, who had already condemned the Revolution in private for introducing religious toleration and the freedom of the press, denied them the latter. In consequence the great majority of the bishops and about half the parish priests refused the oath to the Civil Constitution and the Assembly ordered them to be replaced. Although the deputies failed to realize it at the time, they had split the country in two and enormously reinforced the opponents of the Revolution.

Religious violence: Catholic peasants attack the National Guard at Montauban

The constitution that was intended to form the roof over all this rebuilding was in fact the only aspect of the Assembly's work that did not endure. Within a year it had been swept away. It provided for a division of power, along the lines that Montesquieu had advocated, between an executive appointed by and responsible to the king, and a legislature made up of a single chamber, elected for two years. To the indignation of radicals like Robespierre, the franchise was restricted to men who paid the equivalent of three days' wages in taxation. This was not democracy, but it was not far off – at least from the male viewpoint. An electorate of something like four or five million was far wider than the rest of Europe could boast. Universal suffrage would not have made much practical difference, since the great majority of the electorate did not bother to vote – less than 5 per cent went to the polls in the municipal elections in Paris in 1790. More serious than this restriction of the franchise was the fact that indirect election concentrated power in the hands of local notables who had to satisfy quite a stiff fiscal qualification to be eligible as electors.

Institutions help create patterns of social behaviour, but the way in which they function also depends on the kind of society on which they are superimposed. This dual relationship created the France depicted in Balzac's novels which lasted well into the nineteenth century. A social revolution, in the sense of a massive transfer of property from one class to another, was neither intended nor effected. Even during the Terror no layman was expropriated unless he was convicted of emigration or treason. Since Church property was sold in order to raise as much money as possible it could not be made easily available to the poor. When the Assembly tried to help those without much capital, by accepting payment in instalments, this probably helped to force up prices. The result was that the disposal of Church property to the value of about £150 million tended on the whole to reinforce the previous pattern of wealth. Many of those whose offices were suppressed and reimbursed used the money to buy Church land. This accelerated the old tendency of office to serve as a stepping-stone on the road to landownership. It may have been intended to do so, since many of the deputies were themselves office-holders.

This does not mean that the Revolution had little effect on economic relationships. Many peasants refused to pay such manorial dues as had not been abolished after 4 August and all were to disappear by 1793. Conditions in the countryside were also affected by the changes in the law courts. In the past these had almost always taken the part of the seigneurs. The new courts, with their elected judges, behaved very differently. The bias of many of them, together with the effect of the abolition of tithes and the disappearance of some sources of manorial income, may have tipped the balance in favour of landowners and against manorial lords in the endless competition for the ownership of the soil. One cannot generalize about such subtle and complex factors in a country of great regional variations, but the Revolution certainly accelerated the transition from a society in which social and economic relationships were dominated by the division between the Orders to one in which a new rivalry between the relatively rich and the positively poor broke up the unity of the village community. Life became easier for many, if not for the very poor.

The economic consequences of the work of the Constituent Assembly were less marked in the towns. Internal free trade and the destruction of the guilds might have encouraged the growth of capitalism, but their effects were offset by the inflation and the British blockade that came with war in 1793. Trade was depressed by the departure into self-imposed exile of many potential customers and by the reluctance of those who stayed behind to spend in a way that advertised their wealth. The working population of the towns, especially in such centres of the luxury industries as Paris, was probably the section of society that suffered most from the Revolution. To a greater extent than historians have recognized, the popular agitation of 1792–94 was a defensive reaction against a falling standard of living by those who considered the Revolution to be largely their handiwork.

The objective of the Constituent Assembly was not to effect a social revolution but to create a more open society in which opportunities, previously restricted to birth, should now be open to talent as well. To call this a 'bourgeois' society is not very helpful. What was intended was the kind of society that existed in England, where wealth was the junior branch in the family tree of status. What transformed the situation in France was the fact that so many of the nobility opted out rather than compete with men whom they considered social inferiors. The new France was a country of notables rather than of seigneurs, but the seigneur, unless he had made himself particularly unpopular, could become the leading notable if he wished. It would be interesting to know how many members of the first two Orders, like de Fosseux at Arras and the bishop of Bayeux, were elected mayors in 1790. Although there were fewer places in the new courts than in the old, something like a quarter of the old judges were re-elected. In the backward Vendée, the country squires acquired a new popularity as the protectors of the villagers against outsiders who brought in newfangled ideas and bought up Church property. Provincial nobles had more to gain from the abolition of purchase and better prospects of promotion than they stood to lose from the admission of commoners to commissioned rank. When the

Assembly reorganized the navy it left a higher proportion of noble officers than there had been in 1789, although commoners were no longer restricted to the rank of sub-lieutenant.

What the noble did lose was the formal recognition of his qualitative difference from the rest of the population. Noble titles were officially abolished in 1790. It is easy – at least for those who are quite sure that they are free from any suggestion of colour prejudice – to ridicule the pretensions of those who denied the natural equality of man. What is more to the point is to recognize that noble attitudes were sincerely held and had been responsible for much that was courageous and disinterested – 'noble' in fact – as well as for much intolerable arrogance. The refusal of so many to accept a society in which they had nothing to fear and not much to lose, except what they held to be their honour, was one of the main factors in thwarting the Assembly's hopes of achieving their aims by peaceful means.

An unflattering view of the *émigré* forces

In the summer of 1789 only a handful of the Court nobility, led by the King's brother, Artois, and the prince de Condé, had left France. Envied and disliked by the provincial nobles whom they despised, they looked more like refugees than the vanguard of an army of liberation. Once abroad, Artois and his brother, Provence, who joined him in 1791, tried to convince the European Powers that they were unofficial regents for the captive Louis XVI, on whose alleged behalf they tried to organize foreign intervention and domestic revolt. During the next year or two they gained in credibility from their steady reinforcement by disgruntled nobles, especially officers in the armed forces. By 1791 half the army officers had resigned their commissions. Other nobles, like the sensible Ferrières, were strongly critical of those who emigrated. 'The noblesse is lost, utterly lost, by its own fault.... They will fail, as they have always failed. Rely on my word for that. The king and queen seem to have accepted the constitution in good faith; it is in their own interest since the *émigrés* seem to want to place all power in the hands of the comte d'Artois and M. de Condé.' Ferrières had maintained in the previous year that 'the peace of the provinces has always depended on the behaviour of the deputies of the clergy and nobility', and the violent and uncompromising attitude of so many of them continually pushed the Assembly toward more radical policies than it would have liked. The deputies reluctantly defended mutinous crews against their suspect officers and refused to ask the king to repress rural revolts. This in turn disgusted the friends of order, and officers complained with some reason that the politicians had put an end to discipline in the armed forces.

Ferrières was right in thinking that the objectives of most of the *émigrés* were aristocratic rather than royalist. They were still fighting the battles of 1788, and the king and queen were well aware of it. Marie Antoinette wrote to the Austrian Ambassador in the summer of 1791 that the royal family had no intention of being saved by the *émigrés* at the price of a worse enslavement than their present one. This could have provided the basis for a compromise with an Assembly that was virtually unanimous in its desire to preserve the monarchy. Where Ferrières was mistaken was in thinking that the king and queen were prepared to accept the constitution. Like the nobility, they had values of their own which ruled out the possibility of certain compromises. Marie Antoinette thought the constitution too 'monstrous' to last. From her point of view, ungrateful members of the Court nobility like La Fayette had engineered the Revolution. Abetted by middle-class deputies whom she dismissed as 'tramps', they had seduced the loyal commons. Sooner or later – and probably sooner if the Powers understood their own interests – 'there will be a general revolution in all the towns and the restoration of order will cause no problems'. In a memoir to her brother, the Habsburg Emperor, she wrote in September 1791, 'Conciliation is out of the question now. Armed force has destroyed everything and only armed force can put things right'. Unwilling to accept the place reserved for him by the Assembly and suspicious of the *émigrés*, Louis XVI temporized in the hope of eventual foreign intervention. This put him in a thoroughly hypocritical situation. He took the oath to defend the constitution at the same time that his wife was writing to the Austrian Ambassador, 'giving the impression of adopting the new ideas is the safest way of quickly defeating them'. The deputies suspected the truth and dared not entrust the king with the authority that he claimed was necessary to make the constitution work.

These factors determined the political history of the Assembly. Like many of its successors in France, it began on the Left and

Je soutiendrai la Constitution   Je détruirai la Constitution

Louis facing both ways

moved steadily to the Right. The 'abolition of feudalism' and the
Declaration of the Rights of Man, both voted in August 1789, came
at a time when the deputies still thought themselves threatened by
royal absolutism. Once the king had been brought to Paris as a
virtual prisoner, the problem of the deputies was to persuade him to
accept a compromise on terms that would not leave him with enough
power to overthrow the whole settlement. This proved unexpectedly
difficult. Since the Ministers were suspected of working in the royal
interest it was unsafe for any individual or group to open public
negotiations with them. The radical press could be relied on to sniff
treachery in any hint of an overture. The consequent need for
secrecy put anyone who approached the Court at the king's mercy,
since his political reputation would be ruined by exposure. Believing
with some justification that street demagogues like Georges Danton
could easily, if expensively, be bought, the king and queen had
grounds for hoping that a combination of bribery and bluff would

Chomme
De la Cour
1791

Chomme
Du peuple
1789

Froid, tantôt Chaud, tantôt Blanc, tantôt noir;
je maintiendrai, mettre autrefois à Gauche,
disois bon jour et je vous dis bon soir.

'Barnave is as equivocal as the king (see p. 99)

allow them to ride out the storm; but the result of their policy was to leave them with no line of retreat if things went wrong.

Mirabeau, who was both an adventurer and a very shrewd politician, called off his attack on the monarchy toward the end of 1789 when he was convinced there was no danger of a return to absolutism. Although the Revolution seemed to him to be drifting toward anarchy, he saw that it might be used to strengthen the effective power of the monarchy if only the King would separate his own cause from that of the nobility, accept much of the revolutionary legislation – and make Mirabeau his chief advisor. In May 1790 he came to terms with the king who agreed to settle his debts (£10,000), pay him a monthly salary (£300) and make him a grant (£50,000) at the end of the Assembly's session, if his conduct was judged satisfactory. At such a price the Court naturally assumed that they had bought Mirabeau's services and not just his advice. He himself was far too intelligent not to have realized that he was working for people who would give short shrift to his constitutional ideas if once he helped them to recover their lost power. Public opinion became suspicious, and Mirabeau's influence in the Assembly was already declining when he died in April 1791, an act which robbed him of his £50,000.

Mirabeau's disappearance cleared the way for a very different attempt at compromise. This came from the men who had led the Left in 1789, the so-called triumvirate of Barnave, Duport and Alexandre de Lameth. There was no question of these men putting themselves up for sale, but their overtures to the Court in the spring of 1791 did expose them to the almost equally lethal charge of being prepared to sacrifice principle to office. Whether their attempt at a *rapprochement* did, in fact, constitute a 'betrayal' of the Revolution depends on one's view of the situation. It did mean that they soon found themselves the victims of a crisis that was not of their making.

On the night of 20 June 1791, the royal family escaped from Paris and headed for the army on the eastern frontier. Their intention was not to leave France but to establish themselves in a safe military position from which they could invite foreign intervention. They would then mediate between the Powers and the Assembly to secure the king's restoration on his own terms without either civil war or dependence on the *émigrés*. After a dramatic succession of accidents the royal coach was stopped within a few miles of its goal and sent back to Paris. In the long run this escapade completed the destruction of the king's prestige. He became a figure of contempt whom cartoonists were fond of portraying as a pig. The short-term consequences of the flight were, however, very different.

The triumvirs realized at once that if Louis were not to be dethroned he would have to be rehabilitated. Dethronement they

Sa famille Des Cochons ramenée Dans L'étable

excluded as likely to provoke foreign war and drive the Revolution in the direction of radicalism. They therefore induced the Assembly to pronounce that the king had been 'kidnapped', and Barnave, one of the three commissioners sent to escort the royal party back to Paris, took advantage of the opportunity to open negotiations with the queen. It was reasonable to suppose that a humiliated and dis-credited monarch would at last realize the futility of his opposition to the Revolution. The triumvirs hoped that a few concessions over the revision of the constitution would lay the basis for a compromise that would give them control over a genuinely constitutional monarchy. Louis XVI issued a statement to the effect that his travels had convinced him of his mistake in thinking the Revolution enjoyed little support. The Assembly then suspended his powers until the constitution should be completed and he could be given the choice between accepting it or abdicating.

Unfortunately for the triumvirs their disingenuous manœuvres provoked the fury of radical opinion in Paris, led by popular clubs, of which the most important was the Cordeliers. Most of the support for this campaign came from working people, who were now beginning to be known as *sans-culottes* (because they wore trousers, rather than knee-breeches or *culottes*). There had been some labour agitation in Paris shortly before the king's flight and economic discontent may have reinforced what was, on the surface, a purely political campaign in favour of a republic. Contemporaries were well aware that this was a revolt of the *sans-culottes* against their

The pigs brought back to the sty; the apprehension of the royal family at Varennes des-troyed the prestige of the king

The 'massacre of the Champ de Mars'

social superiors. Both the Assembly and the Paris Commune were determined to make no concessions, if not actually seeking a pretext for a show of force. On 17 July the murder of a couple of Peeping Toms, although not directly connected with the republican petition that was being prepared, provided an excuse for the proclamation of martial law. National Guards sent to disperse the petitioners opened fire and killed about a score of them. Contemporary reports bring out the social nature of the confrontation very clearly. Gouverneur Morris thought the incident would help restore order, although stronger measures would probably be needed against the 'abominable populace'. The king's sister observed that the victims were 'sans-culottes' and the National Guards 'bourgeois' who 'are very keen to be rid of the tramps who are behind the agitation'.

This 'massacre' of the Champ de Mars produced what the British Ambassador called a 'wonderful change' in the situation. Martial law remained in force for weeks, suspects were arrested and radical leaders like Danton and Camille Desmoulins left the capital or went into hiding. The Jacobin club broke up and almost all the deputies who had been members left to form a new club at the Feuillants, leaving Robespierre and his colleague, Jérôme Pétion, among the wreckage. For the first time since 1789 the impetus of the Revolution had been abruptly checked and the first signs of the emergence of a popular movement had seen the National Guard align itself with the forces of order.

For the triumvirs, or the Feuillants, as their party came to be called, this was rather too much of a good thing. They probably enjoyed the discomfiture of those who had been taunting them with betraying the Revolution, but their own position was untenable. The majority of the Assembly was too suspicious of the Court to accept any substantial amendment to the constitution; and the queen, while inviting their advice, had no intention of following their suggestions. It was only a matter of time before Barnave realized she was merely playing with him. By the end of the year the Feuillant policies were discredited, and with their eclipse went the last chance of preserving some sort of constitutional monarchy.

Their failure saw the revival of the radicals, which meant those who had remained attached to the principles of 1789 when the Feuillants were prepared to make concessions to the Court. The most prominent of these was Robespierre, of whom his colleague, Dubois-Crancé, wrote: 'After the death of Mirabeau, the defection of the *patriote* party and the treason of the Lameths, Robespierre showed great strength of character and, in spite of the extreme unpopularity of his views, he won the respect even of his enemies.' He and Pétion received a popular ovation when they left the last session of the Assembly on 30 September. The *patriotes* of 1789 were now badly divided, with the *sans-culottes* and a handful of radical deputies separated from the majority of the Assembly by the bloodshed on the Champ de Mars. With the former leaders of the Left increasingly discredited, the king had made an extraordinary recovery from his apparently desperate position after his flight.

Danse qu'ils Danseront   Lat.

Pas de Deux entre un Jacobin et un Feuillant

How the royalists proposed to treat both Feuillants and Jacobins

CHAPTER FIVE

The breakdown of authority: October 1791–June 1793

Opposite The cost of storming the Tuileries

The reorganization of France by the Constituent Assembly was an attempt to bring French institutions into harmony with the demands of efficient government and a nascent capitalist economy. It assumed that men elected to office would exercise authority in accordance with liberal theories common to most of those brought up in the intellectual atmosphere of the Enlightenment. This is not to say that the Revolution transferred political power to a bourgeois class already in control of the means of production. Land was still the main source of wealth; much of it remained in noble hands and the Revolution did little to alter people's attitudes to landownership. Before 1789 there had not been any ruling class, since the nobility – who were not an economic class in any case – had exercised no political power, and such authority as Parlements and Provincial Estates had retained was largely negative. What the Assembly did was to create the basis for a system in which political power would have been entrusted to men who already possessed wealth or social status, irrespective of whether they were nobles or commoners.

The refusal of the royal government and of many nobles to accept the compromise offered them wrecked the entire experiment. International war, which was eventually accepted by the majority in every camp as the only way out of the stalemate, created a new situation in which the forcible restoration of aristocratic or royal power became a serious possibility. The ensuing crisis divided the revolutionaries of 1789 and forced all of them into false positions. Those determined to defend the Revolution, their careers and – in the case of men who voted for the king's death – their lives, found themselves increasingly driven to rely on popular support. This involved making at least temporary concessions to the demands of the *sans-culottes* for the revival of the traditional economic controls, which gave consumers some protection against inflation and dearth. It also meant, at the height of the Terror, entrusting some police powers (although very little political power) to men whom the revolutionary leaders considered too ignorant to use them properly. The result was to create understandable, if excessive, fears that the rights of property were in danger and the whole social order threatened with collapse. Those who, standing by their principles, rejected tactical concessions, were impelled by their emphasis on order and resistance to *sans-culotte* pressures, toward policies that looked increasingly like those of the avowed counter-revolutionaries and that would, in fact, probably have led to military defeat. Individual ambitions and suspicions prevented the leaders from understanding what was happening. Each side, genuinely convinced that its opponents were betraying the principles of 1789, attacked the other with such ferocity that the state machinery itself came near to breaking down.

Conviction, as well as the lack of effective power, led revolutionary governments to prefer exhortation to coercion. Pétion, the President of the Assembly in October 1792, wrote to the naval authorities in Brest, where the crew of the *Patriote* had just mutinied against their captain: 'I invite Captain Landais to treat his crew with all the mildness that the law recommends toward free men and I invite the brave seamen . . . to remember that ships of war depend for their force on subordination and mutual confidence. Inform them therefore, my dear fellow-citizens, that unless they behave well in the future . . . I shall be obliged to report them to the Convention.' This was not how the British treated mutineers in wartime. Up to a point, the appeal to *fraternité* succeeded, and people all over France responded to the exhilaration of a new order of things in which the man in office exchanged the title of Monseigneur for that of Citizen Minister. But revolutionary camaraderie was not enough to surmount desperate military danger, internal division and the corrosive suspicions arising from both. Governments drifted from one crisis to another under the battering of Allied offensives and widespread civil war.

October 1791 saw the opening of the session of the Legislative Assembly. This consisted of a moderate majority, hoping for a compromise with the king, and a radical wing, somewhat misleadingly known as Brissotins and subsequently as Girondins, although they did not recognize Brissot as their leader and only a few had been elected in the coastal department of the Gironde. All were new men, since the Constituent Assembly, on Robespierre's motion, had declared its members to be ineligible. The Girondin group contained men who had been active in local politics and a handful of Parisians, mostly editors of revolutionary newspapers. They were eager for office and confident that they could use the Assembly to force the king into accepting both their policies and their services. They induced the majority to vote for the deportation of priests who refused the oath to the Civil Constitution of the Clergy and to demand the death penalty for *émigrés* who refused to leave the expeditionary force that had been created on German soil. These were the first terrorist measures voted during the Revolution and they would probably not have passed in the Constituent Assembly. The

Vergniaud, the voice of the Gironde

language of one of their supporters, Maximin Isnard, shows how the political climate had become more harsh. 'All caution is weakness; the bravest heads are the best and an excess of firmness is the guarantee of success . . . we must cut off the gangrened limb to save the rest of the body.' Both proposals were vetoed by the king.

Brissot then turned to the idea of a limited war as a means of forcing the king to accept political defeat. He thought that revolutionary armies would be welcomed as liberators in Germany, the *émigrés* dispersed and their supporters in France – both in the Tuileries palace and in the country at large – driven to come to terms with the Revolution. Brissot's speeches in the Jacobin club and the Assembly, supported by a vigorous press campaign, whipped up a good deal of popular enthusiasm for war. By the spring of 1792 most influential opinion was in favour. The king and queen were confident that Allied armies would brush aside the French forces and restore them to their former power. Ambitious men like the comte de Narbonne, the Minister of War, and La Fayette, who had been given command of an army, hoped to use their positions in order to force their own arbitration on both king and Assembly.

Republican troops leaving for the front

It was precisely this general agreement that worried some members of the Jacobin club. Robespierre was soon convinced that a policy so eagerly taken up by the Court, and by the man whose National Guards had fired on the crowd at the Champ de Mars, could not be in the interests of the Revolution. The situation became more complicated in March 1792 when Louis XVI appointed three of the Girondins, Roland, Clavière and Lebrun, to be his Ministers. War was declared on Austria in the following month and Prussia came to Austria's support. The Girondins understandably called for national unity and the enforcement of discipline in the armies – even if one of them was led by La Fayette. Their Jacobin opponents objected that victory would put military power in the hands of their enemies, and that defeat, which they thought much more likely, might well destroy everything the Revolution had achieved. They went on to draw the unwarranted conclusion that Brissot and his friends realized this too, and were betraying the Revolution in the hope of negotiating a private deal with the Court. Brissot and the Girondin press hit back equally unfairly, accusing Robespierre and his political allies of being defeatist royal agents. This vicious conflict completely paralysed the Jacobin club. Neither side was to forget either the abuse or the suspicion and, although some individuals subsequently changed sides, the breach was never healed. In the meantime the military campaign opened disastrously. The French armies fell back at the first sign of opposition, troops murdered their officers and whole units deserted. The royal family, while apprehensive about their personal safety, could feel reasonably pleased with the way in which the situation was developing.

The king was certainly confident enough to dismiss the three Girondin Ministers when Roland presumed to criticize his policies. That was on 12 June; on 20 June the Girondins organized a popular demonstration that broke into the Tuileries. Louis, who was not lacking in passive courage, refused to be intimidated into any political concessions, and the immediate result of the incident was a certain movement of moderate opinion in his favour. For the time being, the dismissal of the Girondin Ministers reunited the Jacobins. Both wings joined in an attack on La Fayette, who left his army to come to Paris, apparently in the hope of enlisting the support of the majority of the Assembly against the 'anarchists', and perhaps of leading the National Guards against the Jacobins. Marie Antoinette, who thought him more dangerous than the democrats, helped to foil this plan and the king rejected La Fayette's offer to get him away from Paris.

During the second half of July it became obvious that a crisis was imminent. The Prussian army was nearing the French frontier and, at the suggestion of the Court, its commander-in-chief, the

The demonstration of 20 June 1792

Duke of Brunswick, issued a manifesto threatening the deputies with trial by court martial if the royal family was not immediately liberated, and Paris itself with military occupation and 'exemplary and unforgettable revenge' if there was any move against the Tuileries. The Court was still playing for all or nothing. In the meantime National Guard units from the provinces, notably from Brest and Marseilles (the latter marching to the song that was named after them) converged on Paris. Officially they were on their way to the front, but they were determined not to leave the capital until it had been made safe for the Revolution. The forty-eight Sections into which the city was divided for electoral purposes had turned themselves into political clubs which, meeting every night, created a central committee to concert action with the provincial National Guards or *fédérés*. The Sections began threatening a march on the Assembly unless it suspended the king and dismissed La Fayette. Pétion, who as mayor of Paris could not afford to back the wrong side, played for time; but the Quinze-vingts Section of the radical faubourg Saint-Antoine, in the east end of Paris, announced that it would take up arms if the king had not been dethroned by midnight on 9 August.

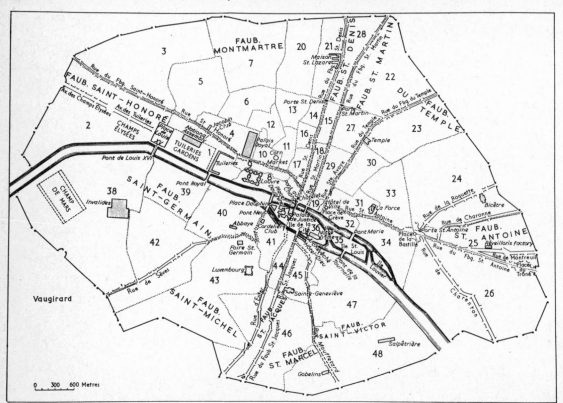

MARCHE DES MARSEILLOIS

CHANTÉE SUR DIFERANS THEATRES

Chez Frere Passage du Saumon

10 August 1792: the crowd
invades the Assembly

It was about this time that one or two of the Girondins made a last
attempt to strike a bargain with the king. Their intention was no
doubt honourable enough but their tactics were singularly inept.
Louis, with liberation in sight, had no intention of becoming their
puppet and was content to temporize. The Girondins tried to
prevent what they regarded as the unnecessary gamble of an insurrection, and threatened to charge Robespierre with sedition. Punctually
at midnight on 9–10 August the tocsin rang. The Sections mobilized
their National Guards, the *fédérés* stood to arms and the Paris
municipality, or Commune, was overthrown and replaced. Pétion
solved his personal dilemma by arranging for his own arrest. In the
early morning the citizens' militia – there was no question of the
'Paris mob' so dear to some British opinion – moved on the Tuileries.
The palace was powerfully defended by Swiss Guards and several
hundred royalist volunteers, and its garrison had the advantage of
fighting under cover. In the opinion of Barbaroux, a Marseillais in
close touch with the *fédérés* of his home town, Louis would have
won if he had personally led the defence. Instead he allowed himself to be persuaded to take his family to the protection of the

Assembly before the fighting began. He did not, however, counter-
mand the orders for the defence of the Tuileries. The first attack
of the *fédérés* was repulsed, but the Parisian National Guards
helped them to eventual victory and the palace was taken, with
losses of several hundred on each side.

The battle of 10 August was the decisive turning-point of the
Revolution, bringing the years of compromise and equivocation to
an abrupt close. The *douceur de vivre* that Talleyrand associated with
the *ancien régime* disappeared overnight as the Insurrectionary
Commune ordered house arrests to seize arms and suspects. Constitutional monarchists went into hiding. For the next month there
was a real reign of terror in Paris, exercised by the *sans-culottes* against
those who had been treating them with contempt only a month
before. The political situation was confused and dangerous. The
moderate majority of the Assembly kept away and the Girondins
dominated the remaining rump. This time they made a clean sweep

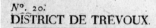

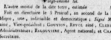

Emigré property is confiscated and sold

The *sans-culottes* as they saw themselves

of ministerial office, except that they thought it wise to offer the Ministry of Justice to Danton, who had played a leading part in the organization of the insurrection. With Danton's promotion, his old clientele from the Cordeliers began to enjoy the spoils of revolution. He created posts for Philippe Fabre d'Églantine and Desmoulins, and offered another to Robespierre who refused it. The Assembly ordered the election as soon as possible of a new constituent body, the Convention, by universal male suffrage and suspended the king until the new assembly should meet. In the meantime the Girondins rushed through a programme of radical legislation. Refractory priests were deported, *émigré* property sold, as far as possible in small lots so that the poor could buy, and surviving manorial dues were abolished without compensation unless the beneficiaries could prove that they related to transfers of land.

The Jacobin opponents of Brissot and his friends were naturally incensed that an insurrection which the Girondins had tried to prevent should have put them in power. The Insurrectionary Commune claimed that it was more representative of public opinion than a discredited and moribund Assembly. Its demand for the creation of a revolutionary court to try those responsible for the bloodshed of 10 August was resisted; when the court that was eventually conceded proved disappointingly lenient, the Commune began to threaten the Assembly. It had very little control over the Sections, and neither the inclination nor the authority to offer concessions. Relations with the Assembly degenerated into open hostility with Robespierre, as the Commune's spokesman, threatening the deputies with the wrath of Paris. The deputies ordered the election of a new Commune but repealed this when the military situation became critical.

Prussian troops crossed the frontier in mid-August. The fortified towns of Longwy and Verdun, which should have held them up until the end of the campaigning season, each capitulated within days, giving rise to plausible suspicions of treason. Only a scratch French army, reinforced by National Guards with more enthusiasm than training, stood between them and Paris. On 2 September the Parisian authorities stuck up melodramatic posters to stimulate recruiting: 'To arms, citizens! The enemy is at our gates.' Some people may have taken this literally. The citizens were summoned to their Sections where they were exhorted to leave for the front. In this feverish situation some men, incited by Marat's newspaper and possibly prompted by the Commune's *comité de surveillance* to which Marat had been irregularly co-opted, began a prison massacre of priests, political suspects and common law prisoners. Some of those responsible probably believed the rumours of a royalist plot to force the prisons and recruit their inmates to a counter-revolutionary force that would hold Paris until the Prussians arrived. Neither the

Appealing for volunteers

The September massacres

Assembly nor the Commune, which knew better, made any serious attempt to stop the butchery until its main force was spent and between 1,000 and 1,500 men and women had been murdered. As Levasseur, one of the men elected to the Convention, explained in his memoirs, to have done so would have meant calling out the National Guard and repeating the experience of the Champ de Mars in the previous year. He was convinced this would have broken the popular *élan* that seemed to him the only hope of keeping out the Prussians.

At the time the Girondins did nothing, even though Roland was Minister of the Interior. Soon, however, they began to exploit the revulsion against the massacres to discredit both Paris and its Commune. Their hatred of popular violence in the capital was a product of the tactical situation – they had not had any scruples about trying to use Parisian violence for their own ends as recently as 20 June. Some of them had excellent personal reasons for their change of mind, since Robespierre and Billaud-Varenne had tried to have

Brissot arrested when men in the gaols were being hacked to death, and a warrant had been issued for the arrest of the Minister of the Interior himself.

The elections to the Convention ensured that this political vendetta would continue. The Jacobins skilfully managed those in Paris, of whose twenty-four deputies sixteen had been associated with the Commune: no less than eleven came from a single Section, Théâtre Français, the home of the Cordeliers and Danton's fief. These Parisian deputies formed the core of the group that, because they sat on the highest seats in the riding school where debates were held, became known as the Montagnards. The elections in the provinces returned a mixture of national celebrities and local favourites. All of the Girondin leaders were successful. The great majority of the provincial deputies however, like Levasseur, did not even know that the republicans were divided into two hostile factions. Some of them gravitated toward the Montagnards or the Girondins, but most remained aloof from both.

During the first weeks of the session the Girondins succeeded in presenting themselves as the party of government. They controlled the ministries – Danton resigned in order to take his seat in the Assembly – and all the major committees except that of General Security, or police. Danton himself was eager to work with them. Instead of leaving well alone they attacked Marat as the chief of the *septembriseurs*, Robespierre as a would-be dictator and Danton as a man who had used his office to line his pockets. Their attempt to have the three men expelled from the Assembly was unsuccessful, but it did mean that the Convention was crippled from the start by its own internal divisions.

The interrogation of a suspect during the prison massacres

In the meantime the military situation had taken an extraordinary turn. Halted at Valmy on 20 September, the Prussian army, ravaged by disease, retreated to the frontier. Within a month the French were in Mainz and Frankfurt. In November they defeated the Austrians at Jemappes and occupied most of Belgium. Farther south they overran Savoy and took Nice, both of which were soon annexed with a good deal of local support. It looked as though Brissot had been right when he claimed that revolutionary armies would prove irresistible. These remarkable successes gave the Convention a free hand to follow its own inclinations. On the whole both Girondins and Montagnards favoured a return to normal government after the exceptional measures of the summer. The revolutionary court was wound up and all restrictions lifted from the corn trade. Roland and Saint-Just, the young Montagnard deputy, extolled the merits of economic liberalism. Robespierre was rather more old-fashioned and favoured controls on the corn trade in order to protect the consumer. Girondins and Montagnards shared in the general over-confidence, and there was no serious opposition to the decision to introduce revolutionary legislation into occupied Belgium (suggesting its eventual annexation) and to offer support to any people struggling for its freedom. Early in 1793 France declared war on the three maritime powers, England, Spain and Holland.

The Allies discomfited

RENTRÉE JOYEUSE ET TRIOMPHANTE DES DON-QUICHOTTES PRUSSIENS EN ALLEMAGNE, APRÈS LA CONQUÊTE DE LA FRANCE, SOUS LA CONDUITE DE L'AIGLE AUTRICHIEN

119

The Temple, where the royal family was imprisoned

The king's farewell to his family

Opposite The execution of Louis XVI

The widowed queen

The one issue that did divide the deputies – apart from their personal quarrels – was the fate of the king. Saint-Just, supported by Robespierre, argued that this was a political rather than a judicial matter. A fair trial would involve the possibility of his acquittal, in which case the insurrection of 10 August would become an unjustified act of rebellion! The Convention nevertheless preferred a trial to the brutal alternative of ordering the king's execution. The Girondins, while agreed that the king was guilty (even before his trial), were divided about the penalty that should be imposed and the desirability of submitting his fate to a referendum. Some of them gave the impression that their main concern was to save his life, with a view to his eventual restoration. The trial itself was an unedifying business. The deputies voted in public, which gave plenty of scope for the intimidation of some and the bribery of others. On 17 January the majority voted for the death penalty, and four days later the king was executed in what is now the Place de la Concorde.

A Party of the Sans Culottes

For Robespierre the verdict was an indication that the Girondins had lost their majority in the Convention and he began to hope that if they could be relegated to the opposition, the way would be clear to provide France with firm but moderate leadership. In February 1793, however, all deputies received a sharp reminder that the *sans-culottes* had opinions of their own. The vigorous prosecution of the war was demanding a degree of mobilization that an eighteenth-century economy found hard to sustain. In January the conscription of 300,000 men was voted, together with an ambitious naval building programme of twenty-five ships of the line and twenty frigates. The strengthening of both army and navy continued for the next eighteen months, until France's land forces outnumbered those of all her opponents put together and the Republic had more ships of the line than England, operating in the Western Approaches. The expenditure necessary for armaments on this scale could not have been covered by taxation even if taxes had been paid regularly and, in many areas at least, they were not. Since 1790 the government had been issuing paper money (assignats) backed by the security of the Church property, and it financed the war effort by printing more and more paper. This meant that metallic currency was hoarded and prices rose. Paris itself was shielded from the worst consequences of inflation, since bread was heavily subsidized; but supplies were not always adequate and even the *sans-culottes* did not live by bread alone. With the stagnation of the luxury trades creating unemployment, they were hit both ways. One of the observers for the Minister of the Interior wrote to him in the spring of 1793: 'This class has suffered a great deal since the revolution; it is the class that took the Bastille, carried through August 10th etc. It is also the class that has

A British view of *sans-culotte* troops

filled the public galleries in assemblies of every kind, that has proposed motions, formed crowds – that has done nothing. Consequently the woman who had a watch, ear-rings, rings, jewels, has pawned them and they have been sold.' It was people of this kind, especially the women, who began to respond to the calls for direct action by new leaders, such as the priest, Jacques Roux. Contemporaries called them 'Enragés'.

Most of those who followed Roux and the Enragé leaders were more concerned with the standard of living than with political niceties. They showed an impartial dislike of both Girondins and Montagnards, and a petitioner to the Assembly was heard making unkind remarks about deputies like Saint-Just, who ate well every night. On 25–26 February crowds stormed the grocers' shops and sold off their contents at prices that seemed fairer to the rioters than to the grocers. Some of the Sections were not unsympathetic but the Commune, whose leaders aspired to play an important role in national politics, regarded the Enragés as a nuisance if not as dangerous competitors. The Girondins saw the whole business as confirming their view that Paris was a nest of anarchy. The Montagnards, who regarded themselves as the natural spokesmen of the *sans-culottes*, resented anyone who took away their clientele. Robespierre went farther. He had been warning the Jacobins that the Girondins would try to provoke disorder to give them a pretext for repression, and the food riots struck him as suspect. Some 'popular movements' did, in fact, look rather odd. An abortive insurrection on 10 March, denounced by both the Commune and the Jacobins, may have been intended to discredit the Revolution. One of its leaders, Desfieux, had previously received money from the king, and

Republican troops bombard Lyons

his subsequent career showed him to be either an incorrigible meddler or a counter-revolutionary tool. Since the Revolution had done so little for the *sans-culottes* their protests could assume almost any political shape. During the spring and summer of 1793 there were municipal revolutions in several of the main provincial towns – Lyons, Bordeaux, Marseilles, Caen and Toulon – which, in some cases, put royalists in control. It is too simple to write off Montagnard suspicion of the Enragés as a product of class antagonism.

The political situation was further complicated by another abrupt change in the military fortunes of the Republic. The enforcement of conscription set off a major civil war in the west. Considerable areas passed out of republican control, and it was largely a matter of luck that the rebels never managed to seize a port where British reinforcements could land. Dumouriez, the commander-in-chief on the northern front, was defeated at Neerwinden on 18 March and evacuated Belgium. He then negotiated an armistice with the Austrians and tried without success to persuade his army to march on Paris. The French were forced out of the Rhineland, leaving an army besieged at Mainz. With a long campaigning season ahead, things looked even blacker than in the previous summer.

The Convention replied to these different threats by voting measures that were later to provide the basis for revolutionary government. A Committee of Public Safety was created to supervise the Ministers,

Opposite A representative of the Convention on mission

A revolutionary club at Toulon

and a revolutionary tribunal for the summary judgment of traitors. *Comités de surveillance* were created in every commune and every Section of the bigger towns. Originally intended merely to keep an eye on foreigners, they quickly began to act as agents for repression of every kind. Necessity got the better of principle and the Convention voted to control the price of grain. The new institutions made little difference to the immediate situation. The revolutionary tribunal gave a fair hearing to the handful of people it tried, most of whom it acquitted. The Committee of Public Safety had little authority.

Some historians have tried to present the rivalry between Girondins and Montagnards as a class issue. By the spring of 1793 the former were certainly denouncing the Parisian *sans-culottes* as anarchists and appealing to the wealthy to join them in the defence of property. The Montagnards proclaimed themselves the natural leaders of the *sans-culottes*, although the sentiment was not necessarily reciprocated. Both attitudes, however, were largely a product of the tactical demands of the political situation. The Girondins had preached violence when they thought they could profit from it, and the Montagnards remained opposed to anything more than temporary concessions to the economic demands of working people. Nevertheless, even though the rivalry of the two groups was mainly due to personal feuds dating from their conflicting attitudes to the war in the previous year, it was bitter enough to make co-operation impossible. The resulting deadlock paralysed the Convention and interfered with the vigorous prosecution of the war. Since the king's trial the Montagnards had seemed to be winning control of the Assembly, but they were weakened by the inclusion of many of their supporters among the scores of political commissars who were sent into the provinces, and the Girondins recovered their self-confidence. With the Republic already in grave military danger this was a situation that could not last long.

Danton made a last effort at reconciliation with the Girondins but, when they accused him of being the tool of Dumouriez, self-preservation drove him to seek their destruction. Robespierre was convinced that the Revolution could only be saved by strong Montagnard government and that this would never be accepted by the Girondins. The problem was what to do. He probably regarded an insurrection against the Girondins as legitimate; but an unsuccessful rising would destroy all his hopes. Leaving the initiative to the *sans-culottes* might lead to the massacre of a good many deputies, the ruin of the Convention and civil war between the revolutionaries. As usual in times of crisis, he advocated a policy of wait-and-see, which led disgruntled *sans-culottes* in the public galleries of the Jacobins to denounce any appeal for moderation as '*du Robespierre*'.

In May the Paris Sections were ordered to provide new recruits to fight in the unpopular civil war in the west. The result was to pack their meetings as all parties tried to secure control over the machinery of recruitment. As the moderates turned up in unaccustomed strength, the political balance swayed to and fro in many Sections. It was just this kind of situation that reversed political control in some of the provincial towns. In the meantime an obscure group of extremists, including a surprising number of foreigners – it was the Montagnards themselves who were later to accuse them of counter-revolutionary intentions – was planning an insurrection. The Girondins declared the Convention to be in danger and the deputies created a Commission of Twelve to deal with plots in Paris. The Commission promptly arrested J. R. Hébert, deputy *procureur* of the Commune and editor of the *Père Duchesne*, a newspaper popular with the *sans-culottes*. Although popular pressure secured Hébert's release, the hitherto cautious Jacobins may well have felt that it was no longer safe to temporize. They seem to have encouraged the attempt of the Paris Department to organize an *insurrection morale* – whatever that was – for 31 May.

If we knew exactly what happened between 31 May and 2 June much of the subsequent history of the Revolution would be a good deal clearer. It looks as though the extremist group that set off the rising on 31 May was trying to forestall the Department and the Jacobins. The insurgents dismissed the Commune – in accordance with the precedent of 10 August – but then reinstated it as a newly consecrated organ of the popular will. The original leaders were then absorbed by the *insurrection morale* group, and the Commune,

reconsecrated or not, showed more interest in the brake than the accelerator. The Sections mobilized their National Guards but did not know what to do with them. Those of Saint-Antoine almost got themselves involved in a battle with the conservative Butte des Moulins. No one knew what was happening and it was a Girondin deputy who persuaded the Assembly to vote its thanks to the Sections. The advocates of restraint had been so successful that the only result of the day's activities was the dissolution of the Committee of Twelve.

When 1 June passed without anything more than large-scale demonstrations, there were signs of discontent among the Montagnards and it looked as though the whole business might peter out. The Commune then took control of the situation. On 2 June petitioners once more demanded that the Convention arrest the leading Girondins and the Twelve. One or two Girondins, including Isnard, volunteered to suspend themselves, which enabled them to survive the Terror and allowed them to take their revenge on the Montagnards in 1795. The majority rejected any such capitulation and the Convention was wondering what to do when it found itself surrounded by National Guards. Beyond the citizens' militia was a large crowd whose intentions remain a mystery. The deputies, in solemn procession, tried to break through the cordon of National Guards but were turned back by Hanriot, the new commander of the popular forces. They returned to their seats and eventually agreed to vote the provisional arrest of the leading Girondins, the Commission of Twelve and Ministers Clavière and Lebrun. Nobody had been killed, and the fiction that the Convention was a free agent had been preserved after a fashion, although the majority of the deputies were not going to forget how they had been intimidated.

The commander of the Parisian National Guard, Hanriot

One man at least knew what he wanted. Robespierre wrote down his private thoughts some time during the three-day crisis: 'We need one will and one only. It has got to be either republican or royalist. To make it republican we need republican Ministers, republican newspapers, republican deputies, a republican government. The foreign war is a mortal disease so long as the body politic suffers from revolutionary sickness and the division of wills. The danger in the interior comes from the bourgeois. To overcome the bourgeois we must win the support of the people.' The history of the next twelve months was to centre on the creation of this unified republican will.

Opposite 2 June 1793: the Convention under pressure from the Parisian National Guard

CHAPTER SIX

The triumph of will:
June 1793–June 1794

The victorious Montagnards thought primarily of safeguarding what had been won rather than of making drastic innovations. They did produce a new constitution that provided for universal male suffrage and the confirmation of laws by referendum, and they completed the long process by which all manorial dues were finally abolished. The Convention was later to tackle the problem of education and try to do something for the sick and aged; but most of the deputies regarded the reorganization of France as already accomplished. When counter-revolution and foreign invasion had been defeated, the way would be open for a return to constitutional government, the rule of law and economic liberalism.

There was, however, more to it than that. Influenced both by circumstances and by the legacy of Rousseau, some Montagnards arrived at a new conception of the nation-state which was entitled to demand the sacrifice of all the private interests of its citizens. The new outlook generated much disinterested self-sacrifice that helped to give revolutionary France its extraordinary strength and its hold over the imagination of contemporaries and future generations. It was also the basis for all kinds of controls and for the ruthless suppression of opposition. The Committee of Public Safety gradually created the kind of war machine that was not seen again until the twentieth century, based on conscription, the direction of labour, the requisitioning of food and scarce materials, government control of shipping and foreign trade, wage and price controls and the systematic use of propaganda. Some of Rousseau's disciples hoped to create a new kind of republican man, conditioned to *vertu* by state education and republican institutions. The transformation of French society that they had in mind was moral rather than economic, and their ideas of moral regeneration coexisted uneasily with conflicting principles of constitutional government and economic liberalism.

What actually happened was the work of practical politicians, many of whom saw the Revolution as a career. This was especially true of those who had used the Cordelier club as an instrument for their advancement. Danton and Fabre d'Eglantine were now wealthy men, unattracted by talk of a new Sparta and impatient to wind up the Revolution. Others, such as Hébert and Vincent, the Secretary-General of the War Office, had been rather less successful.

Opposite Robespierre

Above Fabre d'Eglantine

Above right Saint-Just

Neither had been elected to the Convention and both hoped, by advocating extremist policies, to force their way to the top with *sans-culotte* support. Those interested had plenty of opportunities to make money out of the Revolution, for example by black-mailing bankers or returned *émigrés* looking for false certificates of residence. Agents of the Commune were involved in the forgery business, and some of Danton's friends took part in corrupt financial speculation. In February 1793 Gouverneur Morris had written to George Washington that corruption was so rife that if there were no traitors the enemy must be lacking in common sense. He was not the only man to think along these lines. As yet it is impossible to know how far these suspicions were justified but they were certainly not unreasonable. The Committee of General Security was purged in the autumn of 1793 because it was thought to be corrupt. The Com-mittee of Public Safety seems to have kept its hands clean, but it developed a collective governmental mentality that did not make it popular in the Convention. Its members were accused of taking on the airs of the old royal Ministers and they were increasingly inclined to treat criticism of the government as unpatriotic.

Opposite Danton

One of the most striking aspects of the period was the extent to which relatively simple people found themselves in positions of local power. *Sans-culotte* militants were likely to be master-craftsmen with some smatterings of education, rather than wage-earners, but they had neither the attitudes nor the manners of gentlemen. Their curious compound of ancient millenarian dreams and the forms and stilted vocabulary of obsessional bureaucracy was to be long remembered, either as an inspiration or a warning. *Sans-culotte* power, however oppressive to its victims, was a precarious and ephemeral matter. In the countryside it depended on support from higher quarters. Girondins in Evreux invited the *sans-culottes* to 'choose between Liberty, which does not even give you water to drink, and ourselves who provide you with a livelihood'. Only the coercive power of the central government could maintain a situation in which tenants dominated their landlords. Even in Paris, where the Convention was at the mercy of street demonstrators, once the Committee of Public Safety consolidated its power it was able to dictate its own terms.

The year that followed the overthrow of the Girondins saw the emergence of the Committee of Public Safety as a War Cabinet. It was responsible to the Convention which voted every month on the renewal of its membership, and its powers were not unlimited. It never controlled finance and it shared its police powers with the Committee of General Security. With these exceptions it came to exercise a virtual dictatorship. Like most War Cabinets, it was a coalition government, ranging from conservatives, such as the military engineers Carnot (who had even protested against the expulsion of the Girondins) and Prieur de la Côte d'Or, to ideological radicals like Saint-Just and Billaud-Varenne. It had no prime minister and its domination by Robespierre is a myth, invented after his death by former colleagues eager to escape blame for unpopular policies. Robespierre's position on the committee was admittedly exceptional. He had no departmental responsibilities and his value to his colleagues arose mainly from his personal prestige, which strengthened their standing in the Convention and the Jacobins. He acted as the committee's ideological spokesman – a role to which Billaud-Varenne also aspired – in defining the objectives of revolutionary government. His colleagues had no inhibitions about challenging him, but relations within the committee seem to have been reasonably cordial until the end of 1793. Robespierre, like most of his colleagues, but with the exception of Saint-Just and Billaud-Varenne, hoped to restore normal constitutional government as soon as the military situation allowed. The first objective of them all was to win the war.

In the days after 2 June, when Danton led the committee, it pursued a conciliatory policy, even when most of the Girondin

Robespierre in the Convention on 9 Thermidor

leaders escaped from their house arrest and tried to persuade the provinces to march on Paris. Most of the Departments initially responded but they soon allowed themselves to be reassured by the voting of the constitution. Even Normandy, where an army of sorts actually set out for Paris, was pacified with very little bloodshed. It was reasonable to hope that moderation would do as much in Lyons, Bordeaux and Marseilles. Jacques Roux, however, brutally challenged the impression of confidence and clemency that the Montagnards were trying to generate. On 25 June he denounced their constitution as a fraud because it did nothing for the poor. His call for something like a class war against the rich encountered the united opposition of the revolutionary leadership. The Commune disowned him and a powerful Jacobin deputation induced the Cordeliers to expel him. Roux fought back, but henceforth he was on the defensive and by the autumn he was in gaol.

It was not social problems but the war that put paid to hopes of moderation. Danton's attempts to open peace negotiations had been rejected by Allies confident of victory. Everything went wrong for the Montagnards. They made no headway against the rebels in the Vendée, and the besieged garrison capitulated at Mainz; France was invaded again and the Austrians took Condé and Valenciennes. Lyons was drifting into open revolt and the end of July saw Toulon fall into the hands of 'moderates' who were soon to proclaim Louis XVII as their king. *Sans-culotte* anger was intensified when Marat was murdered by Charlotte Corday on 13 July. Although she had, in fact, acted on her own initiative, she had been in touch with

Marat

Marat murdered by Charlotte Corday

MEMENTO MORI
SACREE CALOTTE.

The *Père Duchesne*, a newspaper edited by Hébert (*below*)

Girondin rebels in Caen, and the Montagnards naturally assumed
that their enemies had turned to political assassination. Marat's death
removed a *sans-culotte* hero who had been a loyal, if irascible,
Montagnard and opened the way for claimants to his succession.
Ambitious for their own advancement, Hébert and Vincent
promptly began attacking Danton and his friends. They did not
share Marat's disinterestedness and they had no respect for a Convention to which they did not belong.

Danton had already been left out of the Committee of Public
Safety when its powers were renewed on 10 July and Robespierre
joined it on 27 July. In August the committee took on the two
military specialists, Carnot and Prieur, who set about the overhaul
of the entire war effort. The Convention added to their problems
on August 23 when it voted the *levée en masse*, conscription of the
eighteen to twenty-five age-group. This was a compromise between
the traditional ways of thinking of the military men and *sans-culotte*
dreams of the entire male population finishing the war in one
irresistible campaign. To provide the hundreds of thousands of new
recruits with arms, munitions, uniforms and food meant the introduction of elaborate controls over manpower and materials. The
naval building programme involved fewer men but huge quantities
of timber, iron, copper, sailcloth, cordage and powder, since the
fleet, unlike the army, disposed of sophisticated and expensive

instruments of war. It took time to set all this machinery in motion and no immediate results were possible.

Toward the end of August the military situation became very bad indeed. The Austrians were established on French soil and the Spaniards across the Pyrenees. British troops, led by the 'noble Duke of York', were besieging Dunkirk while Toulon handed over to the British and Spanish fleets thirty-one ships of the line and twenty-six frigates without a shot being fired. This was the worst disaster in French naval history and proof enough to the *sans-culottes* and militants in general of the Republic's vulnerability to traitors. The Jacobins became increasingly restive, and the government, discredited by defeat, lost control of the political situation. On 4 September a demonstration at the Commune calling for higher wages was diverted by the *procureur*, Chaumette, and his deputy, Hébert, and was persuaded to march on the Convention the next day.

The *journée* of 5 September was too much like the crisis of 31 May–2 June for the comfort of the deputies. This time Hébert and the Commune had deserted the Montagnards. The crowd invaded the Assembly, and when Robespierre's attempt to get all motions referred to the Committee of Public Safety was defeated, the government bowed before the storm and accepted radical measures that it would have preferred to avoid. As these took shape over the next week or two, controls were introduced on both wages and the prices of all necessities. The law of suspects designated – in the vaguest

Sans-culottes making saltpetre for the army

Revolutionary government in
action: (*above*) a *comité révolutionnaire*, and (*right*) the
revolutionary tribunal at Lyons

terms – whole categories of people who could be arrested and kept in prison indefinitely without trial. This put terrible powers in the hands of the *comités révolutionnaires* or *comités de surveillance* of the Sections. Control over these committees became the objective of obscure factional struggles. A 'revolutionary army' was set up to intimidate the opponents of the Revolution, especially those withholding grain from the market. The Committee of Public Safety, which would have liked to put Hanriot in command, had to accept Ronsin, an ambitious man already at loggerheads with some of Danton's followers, and the ally of Hébert and Vincent. Two men associated with popular protest, Collot d'Herbois and Billaud-Varenne, were added to the committee. This ended their opposition for the time being, although both were to come out against Robespierre in the following summer.

Whether from conviction or because it was afraid to do anything else, the committee gave up trying to moderate the revolutionary movement for the time being. As Levasseur described it afterward, 'No one had dreamt of establishing a system of terror. It established itself by force of circumstances; no one's will organized it but everyone's will contributed to its creation.' In Paris one state trial followed another: Marie Antoinette, twenty-one Girondin leaders, Barnave, Madame Roland, Bailly and others went to the guillotine within less than two months. Only Robespierre's opposition prevented another seventy-five Girondins being tried for signing a secret protest against the arrest of their leaders. Some of the deputies sent into the provinces resorted to legalized massacres. These were not

Marie Antoinette on her way to execution

Popular sovereignty in action

necessarily approved by the committee, but it did replace one of its own members (Couthon) at Lyons by another (Collot) on the ground that Couthon was too lenient. The Convention gave these representatives on mission plenipotentiary powers, and the committee urged them to 'electrify' and 'revolutionize' in the most general terms. The result was an outburst of local initiative that put radicals in power over most of France but brought the country to the verge of anarchy. A good many towns created their own revolutionary armies with the intention of commandeering all the available food over as wide an area as possible. Conflicts between rival municipalities and the attempts of local men to frustrate requisitioning for the army threatened to wreck all authority. In the Vendée a superabundance of deputies attached to the numerous armies took up the quarrels of the generals, and the ensuing conflicts were carried back into the Convention. These were the more serious since what might be called a 'Hébertist' military faction in the Vendée, centred on Ronsin and Rossignol, was opposed by a 'Dantonist' faction led by Westermann and Fabre d'Eglantine's brother. No government was likely to tolerate this kind of confusion for long, certainly not the Committee of Public Safety, and it was merely a matter of time before is tried to assert its own authority.

Matters were complicated by the sudden emergence of a new religious conflict in November 1793. The revolutionaries' determination to make all things new and rational – typified by their introduction of the metric system – led to the introduction of a new calendar. The republican era was dated from the abolition of the monarchy on 21 September 1792. The *décade* replaced the week, thereby doing away with Sundays and with the familiar Christian festivals.

At the same time churches were being stripped of bells, bellropes and sacred vessels in the interest of the war effort. Out of all this arose a more positive dechristianization movement, aimed at Catholicism itself. This was a complex and confusing affair, at once a popular movement, an ideological attitude and a political intrigue. A small group of ambitious but obscure politicians, including Desfieux, were trying to create a political machine supported by a federation of the popular societies in Paris. The initiative of these men induced the archbishop of Paris to offer his resignation to the Convention on 7 November. The Commune hastened to jump on this promising bandwagon and organized a festival of Reason in Notre-Dame a few days later. It went on to order the closure of all churches in Paris. Dechristianization came to be adopted as one of the hallmarks of the good *sans-culotte*, and, as the movement spread all over the country, almost all the churches in France were closed and most of the clergy bullied into resigning or abjuring.

The revolutionary calendar combined Reason and *sensibilité*: personifications of Brumaire, Thermidor and (*opposite*) Germinal

The worship of Reason

A Republican magistrate re-unites a divorced couple

The worship of the Supreme Being was a
more solemn affair than the cult of Reason

Republican playing cards

The autumn of 1793 is the most complicated period of the Revolution because so many things were happening at the same time. Most of the men involved played several roles: enemies in one context could be allies in another. Religion, as usual in French politics, cut across political divisions and there were dechristianizers in both the 'Dantonist' and 'Hébertist' camps. While the spontaneous Terror and the anti-religious campaign were still gathering strength in the provinces, yet another turn in the military situation was allowing the Committee of Public Safety to consolidate its authority in the Convention. French victories in September and October threw the British and the Austrians on to the defensive in Belgium. Lyons was recaptured and a Vendean army that had ventured north of the Loire was cut to pieces in December. The Allies were driven out of Toulon in such haste that over half the ships there were saved. Already, on 10 October, the Convention had voted that the government was to remain 'revolutionary' for the duration of the war. This meant that the new constitution was officially shelved and the reign of the Committee of Public Safety prolonged indefinitely. On 4 December a new decree provided revolutionary government with a kind of constitution of its own. The Committees of Public Safety and General Security were given control over all local authorities and representatives on mission. All revolutionary armies raised in the provinces were to be disbanded. This was not to suppress the Terror but to nationalize the terrorist creations of private enterprise. To the extent that *sans-culotte* power had grown up on a local basis, on the initiative of representatives on mission and their agents, the new organization meant that power was transferred back into the hands of the educated gentlemen in the Convention. They were gradually acquiring the means to enforce their own policies, but it was still too soon for anyone to know what these would be. Irrespective of the policies themselves, the committee was sooner or later likely to come up against the ambitious group entrenched in the Paris Commune, the War Office, the Parisian revolutionary army and the Cordeliers – a confrontation that the government viewed with some apprehension.

The unity of the Montagnards had not survived the defeat of their political rivals. No one who reads the debates of the period can fail to be impressed by the emergence of obscure factions and the growth of vicious mud-slinging during the autumn of 1793. Levasseur, on his return from the front, found it very depressing. 'I found [the Convention] so changed that my head swam . . . I could scarcely recognize my colleagues. . . . In the place of that *Montagne* which had formed a single compact and united whole, I discovered a crowd of rival factions which dared not fight each other in the open but waged an underground war that was perhaps more dangerous than

Civil war at Lyons, December 1793

conflicts in debate. In practically all the new parties men of goodwill were in the majority but one also found traces of evil designs and treacherous intentions.' Even writing a generation after the events, he was still convinced that the British government was behind all the intrigue and that Hébert and his allies were in the pay of the counter-revolution.

The extent and nature of British involvement is still an open question. What was perhaps more important at the time is the fact that it was almost universally believed to exist. Levasseur was certainly right in emphasizing that the factions, instead of challenging each other on matters of policy, tried to exploit suspicion and innuendo, together with the formidable repressive machinery of the Terror, in order to destroy their opponents. One powerful motive of discontent was the resentment of some representatives on mission against the government's conduct of the war in the Vendée. After his recall from the west, Bourdon de l'Oise, a hitherto inconspicuous deputy, waged a personal vendetta against the War Minister, J. B. Bouchotte, whose dismissal he demanded at almost fortnightly intervals. Henceforth the enemies of the War Office were Bourdon's friends. Philippeaux returned from the Vendée so incensed that he published a couple of pamphlets accusing the Committee of Public Safety of deliberately sabotaging military operations in that theatre. Hébert, who had been denouncing Danton since the summer, acquired a new grievance when Danton's protégé, Paré, was made Minister of the Interior, a post that Hébert would have liked for himself. Men with a past to live down, like the ex-marquis Maribon-Montaut, sought safety in extremism and the denunciation of *modérantisme*. Financial racketeering complicated these already tortuous relationships. In October, Fabre d'Églantine, who was himself to become fatally involved in the falsification of a decree for the liquidation of the East India Company, secretly denounced to members of the governing committees a 'foreign plot' by a handful of apparent extremists, one of whom was Desfieux. In November, Chabot exposed the East India Company fraud, which he declared to be merely the exposed tip of a whole counter-revolutionary iceberg. Although Robespierre warned him to '*ménager les patriotes*', Chabot incriminated Hébert and Chabot's associate, Basire, made charges against Danton. It is impossible now, as it was then, to know how much of Chabot's story was true. Some of it was at least plausible and it certainly succeeded in poisoning the whole political atmosphere.

One or two of Robespierre's speeches suggest that he thought the turning of the military tide meant that the Revolution was safe at last and the way open for a gradual return to constitutional government. As he saw it, the 'despots', defeated on the battlefield, were playing their last desperate card in the hope that their agents could deceive the revolutionaries into destroying each other. Like Levasseur, he distinguished between a handful of enemy agents and the sincere but gullible deputies whom they were misleading. Throughout the autumn he had patiently defended one Jacobin against another, but he finally arrived at the conclusion that the only way to put an end to the faction fighting was to hunt out the real trouble-makers and destroy them. Fabre's denunciation of Desfieux and his confederates seemed to be confirmed by their leading role in the dechristianization campaign, which offended Robespierre's Rousseauist deism and aroused unnecessary opposition. On 21 November he attacked dechristianization in the Jacobins and had the 'foreign agents', Desfieux, Proli, Pereira and Dubuisson, expelled from the club.

By December these complex feuds and factions had become roughly polarized in a battle between the group that looked to Danton for protection – and possibly for leadership – and the men from the Cordeliers. Danton's own part is obscure, since he liked to remain in the background, but Joseph Garat, the former Minister of the Interior, claimed that Danton told him his policy was to secure an amnesty and the return to the Convention of those Girondins who were under arrest, to make peace, to restore prosperity by winding up the economic controls and to end the police terror. His tactics were to defeat the governing committees in the Convention by an alliance between his followers on the Left and what remained of the Right; to win over Robespierre and Barère, of the Committee of Public Safety; and to replace its more violent members, Saint-Just, Collot and Billaud. This was a policy that was likely to appeal to the majority of the Committee of Public Safety, provided that it was implemented in an orderly fashion so as not to disrupt the war economy until peace had been concluded with some at least of the Republic's many enemies. As Levasseur put it much later: 'Everyone of any merit, Robespierre and Danton, Camille Desmoulins and Saint-Just, realized that the Revolution had reached its peak and all that remained to be done was to regulate it. All wanted to return to *indulgence* and legal order but all took different roads to the same goal.' Robespierre had personally saved the Girondin back-benchers; he and Danton had taken the lead in opposing dechristianization. When Desmoulins, an old friend of them both, launched another newspaper, the *Vieux Cordelier*, to support the policy of moderation, he showed the proofs of the first numbers to Robespierre, who may well have approved of his intentions.

The whole scheme was spoiled by the irresponsibility of Desmoulins and the impatience of Fabre. Carried away by his journalistic success, in his third number (of 15 December) Desmoulins made an undiscriminating attack on the Terror and the Committee of Public Safety. Although Robespierre went on defending him in the Jacobins, he was not prepared to support an attack on the committee to which he belonged. Fabre, aware that it was only a matter of time before the investigation of the scandal of the liquidation of the East India Company exposed his own corruption, was in a hurry to destroy the Cordeliers and intimidate any possible opponents. A parliamentary offensive, designed to change the membership of the Committee of Public Safety, misfired; but on 17 December Fabre induced his fellow-deputies to order the arrest of Vincent, without consulting the Committee of General Security. Bourdon de l'Oise got the motion extended to include Ronsin, his old enemy in the Vendée, who had just returned from duty in Lyons. The campaign for *indulgence* was taking the form of an attack on the Cordeliers.

On 21 December Collot d'Herbois returned from Lyons. Self-preservation, as well as conviction, drove him to take up the defence of Ronsin who had been under his orders. He won over many Jacobins, and Hébert, who had been relatively quiet, plucked up

Desmoulins

enough courage to return to the offensive. It was now too late to think in terms of an alliance between Danton and the majority of the Committee of Public Safety. To preserve its own unity the committee took up a neutral position, treating both *indulgents* and Cordeliers as factious. The arrest of Fabre on 12 January meant that both sides now had hostages in gaol and gave the government a temporary respite. Sooner or later, however, Fabre, Vincent and Ronsin would have to be either released or brought to trial. Any trial would precipitate a crisis, and the victory of either faction might leave the government at the mercy of the other.

The release of Vincent and Ronsin on 1 February led to a predictable offensive from the Cordeliers. After some hesitation and temporary loss of nerve, in early March the leading members of the club began threatening a new 31 May. Collot, as the spokesman of the Jacobins, tried to negotiate a truce but the Cordeliers insisted on the destruction of their rivals. When they continued with their threatening noises the government struck first, ordering their arrest on 13 March. The subsequent trial of Hébert, Vincent, Ronsin and their supporters involved the risk of a violent reaction from the Commune and the Sections. The two governing committees divided the Commune by protecting its mayor, Pache, and Hanriot, the commander of the Parisian National Guard, whom over-enthusiastic witnesses were eager to accuse. The trial itself was a thoroughly artificial business. Some plausible charges against Hébert were not investigated; others were invented in order to discredit the accused in the eyes of the *sans-culottes*: for example, by attributing to them a plot to interfere with food supplies to the capital. As one contemporary put it, 'Hébert, who had committed plenty of real crimes, died for imaginary ones.' Desfieux and his group were put in the dock with the Cordeliers. All the accused were found guilty and executed, with the exception of a police spy.

While the Public Prosecutor, Fouquier-Tinville, was preparing the case against Hébert and his associates, the Convention voted to put on trial the men involved in the East India Company fraud, of whom the most important was Danton's friend, Fabre. When Amar, of the Committee of General Security, tried to present this as a straightforward case of corruption – which would have protected the accused from the revolutionary tribunal and the death sentence – Billaud and Robespierre insisted that it should be treated as a political matter. This immediately raised the question of who was to be included. Fouquier's records indicate that the decision to involve Danton and Desmoulins was taken very late. Billaud and Saint-Just seem to have pressed for it and Robespierre was at first violently opposed. Secret negotiations took place and Danton may have been offered his personal safety if he undertook not to try to persuade the Convention to intervene on behalf of Fabre. If so, he refused. To leave Danton at liberty meant risking one of his impassioned speeches that might swing the Convention; and defeat on an issue of this kind would overturn the government and probably put some of its members in the dock. After some hesitation, Robespierre made up his mind to take an active part in preparing the case against Danton. The trial of the 'Dantonists' was an entirely different matter from that of Hébert. The deputies had no doubt been glad to be rid of the men from the Cordeliers and the Commune who were threatening them; Danton, however, had plenty of friends in the Assembly and, whatever his colleagues thought of his personal reputation, they approved of the moderate policies with which his name was associated. Self-preservation alone would have made them reluctant to send fellow-deputies before the revolutionary tribunal. The government, in the event, got its way in the Convention, but not without some uneasy moments. Danton himself was made of sterner stuff than Hébert. He dominated the trial and won over the audience in the courtroom. It was only by a vigorous policy of deceit and intimidation that the two committees and Fouquier-Tinville were able to tame the Convention and induce the hand-picked jury to bring in a verdict of guilty.

The Committee of Public Safety had probably hoped to handle both the Cordeliers and the *indulgents* by parliamentary means. The pressure of events had forced them into dangerous and bloody expedients, and it was their intention that the purge of deputies should stop at Danton. In fact, they had opened Pandora's box and, to quote the Montagnard, Choudieu, inflicted 'an incurable wound; after this new blow to the nation's representatives there was no end to the proscriptions'. The Convention had been browbeaten into silence, but there were now many Montagnards who regarded the two committees as tyrants and the prospects of any smooth transition to normal constitutional government had been ruined.

In these circumstances the increasing centralization of power in the hands of the Committee of Public Safety had an air of despera-tion about it. The two committees provided all but one of the next seven presidents of the Jacobin club, where all genuine freedom of debate had now been extinguished. The government established a tight control over the Paris Commune. Chaumette was executed, Pache arrested and all the important positions on the Commune filled by nominees of the Committee of Public Safety. The popular societies which were all that was left of an autonomous *sans-culotte* movement were bullied into disbanding. When some of the Sections began to organize fraternal banquets in the streets this premature fraternization was suppressed. The ministries were abolished and the Ministers replaced by civil servants under the immediate control

Un petit Souper, à la Parisienne: —or— A Family of Sans Culotts refreshing, after the fatigues of the day.

The Terror, as seen from across the Channel

of the Committee of Public Safety. All but two of the revolutionary tribunals in the provinces were abolished and prisoners brought to Paris for trial. A savage law of 10 June, the work of Robespierre and Couthon, deprived the accused of counsel and the right to call witnesses. Convictions which, during the winter, had averaged around 30 per cent, increased to over 70 per cent. This was the period of the *Grande Terreur* which left an unforgettable impression on France and Europe.

The bureaucratic ferocity of the government was a sign of weakness rather than of strength. If it could no longer rely on the spontaneous action of the citizens, this was its own doing if not altogether its own fault. *Sans-culottes* suffered as much as anyone else from the new attitudes. When dockyard workers went on strike at Cherbourg against the second reduction in wage rates in less than a year (itself probably the result of a ministerial mistake which the authorities were afraid to report to the Committee of Public Safety), the local authorities at Cherbourg blamed the strike on paid agitators and threatened anyone who failed to return to work at once with denunciation to the Committee of Public Safety as an enemy of the Revolution. This was a far cry from Pétion's homilies. After the execution of extremists and moderates alike, no one knew what was orthodox any more and the fact that the revolutionary movement had lost all sense of direction was one of the reasons for the government's policy of extreme centralization. This process transferred all the tensions and frustrations to the Committee of Public Safety itself. Never had it been so powerful, so isolated and so much hated. The unnatural tension could not continue for long but there was no means of telling how it would end nor who would perish in the inevitable explosion.

The Revolution was a poor time for the arts

CHAPTER SEVEN

The search for stability:
June 1794–November 1799

By the summer of 1794 the problem was how to end the Revolution. What had been achieved was as much as all but a handful of deputies thought to be desirable. The defeat of the Austrians at Fleurus, in mid-June, heralded the last swing of the military pendulum. The republican armies took the offensive on all fronts and, although the Brest fleet suffered a setback in the battle of 1 June, the food convoy from America that it had been sent out to protect arrived safely. There was now no need for the Terror. Most of the Montagnards would have agreed, though perhaps not in public, that it had to be stopped. Even Saint-Just said as much to Levasseur in the privacy of his tent at the front. The problem was how to do it. Within the Committee of Public Safety, Billaud-Varenne seems to have thought of continuing until all French society had been regenerated and Collot d'Herbois knew that any relaxation of the government's grip would expose him to denunciation for the atrocities that he had endorsed at Lyons. If there had ever been any chance of an amnesty and a controlled return to normal government it had vanished with the purges of March and April, which had left many friends and followers of Danton and the Cordeliers appre-hensive for their own safety and eager for revenge. The concentration of all power in the hands of the government made it the focus of all discontents. Small groups of frightened and discontented Monta-gnards began to discuss ways of ending the domination of the Con-vention by the two committees. The Committee of General Security was itself antagonized by the fact that a new police bureau, created within the Committee of Public Safety and directed for most of its brief existence by Robespierre, encroached on its authority. Each committee also suffered from internal factions. Robespierre's enemies within the Committee of General Security tried to strengthen their position by making contact with discontented Montagnard back-benchers, and Robespierre toyed with the idea of appealing over the heads of the Montagnard deputies to the silent majority in the Convention. The sense of fear and insecurity was universal and intolerable.

What brought matters to a head was the growing division within the Committee of Public Safety itself. In this confused conflict of policies and personalities it is impossible to be sure where anyone

Opposite The Republic vic-torious on land (the battle of Fleurus) and defeated at sea (the sinking of the *Vengeur* at the Glorious First of June)

Repression gone mad: Le Bon and the twin revolutionary tribunals at Arras and Cambrai

stood. Most of the evidence comes from those who, after over-throwing Robespierre, tried to save their own lives by blaming him for everything that had happened. It looks as though he and Couthon, eventually supported by Saint-Just, argued that it would be impossible to stop the Terror without first executing half a dozen deputies too closely implicated in the atrocities in the provinces to tolerate any policy of moderation. Billaud and Collot saw no need to stop the Terror at all, and most of the remaining members of the committee – perhaps mindful of the fact that Danton's trial had almost escaped their control – refused to accept any further purge of the Convention. Carnot and Saint-Just were engaged in a private feud about the conduct of military operations, while Robespierre, whose nerves were inclined to let him down in periods of crisis, was a difficult colleague, suspicious of the others and increasingly inclined to commit them to policies about which they had not been consulted.

On 26 July Robespierre precipitated the crisis by demanding that the Convention purge the Committee of General Security, subordinate it to the Committee of Public Safety, and purge that too. The Assembly, after automatically approving his speech, changed its mind and adopted a non-committal attitude. The Jacobins came to his support but their influence was now too slight to matter much. During the night of the 26–27 July desperate negotiations among the Montagnards built up an anti-Robespierrist coalition. On the following day – 9 Thermidor Year II in the revolutionary calendar – Saint-Just tried to persuade the Convention to censure Billaud and Collot, though without excluding them from the committee. He was shouted down and Robespierre was denied a further hearing. After a good deal of noisy vituperation, the Assembly voted the arrest of Robespierre, Couthon and Saint-Just; Robespierre's brother and Le Bas, of the Committee of General Security, who insisted on associating themselves with the three accused deputies, were also arrested. In view of the tendency of Robespierrist historians to identify their hero with the Committee of Public Safety, it is worth emphasizing that, at this stage, the crisis had produced a victory for the majority of the committee, and the result looked like being a continuation of the Terror.

The execution of Robespierre

The situation was transformed when Robespierre's friends in the Paris Commune tried to organize an insurrection in his support. This looked like the confrontation with Paris that the deputies had feared for so long. During the evening both sides competed for the allegiance of the Parisian National Guard, and civil war in the capital seemed imminent. The Commune failed to exploit its initial military superiority and when the Convention outlawed both the rebel deputies and the Commune, support for the insurrection gradually melted away. In the early hours of 28 July National Guards loyal to the Convention occupied the Commune's head-quarters in the Hôtel de Ville without opposition. The victors put to death the five deputies, six officials of the Commune and eighty-seven of its ordinary members. The municipal administration was virtually annihilated and for the first time since 1792 the Assembly was free from any threat of direct action in the streets. This un-expected sequel to the political crisis upset the balance of power, since the deputies no longer needed a strong government to protect them. When the surviving members of the Committee of Public Safety proposed to replace their former colleagues and carry on as before, the Assembly refused. It broke the supremacy of the com-mittee by confining its powers to war and diplomacy, and ordering the rotation of its membership. The unfortunate Fouquier-Tinville, who had only done what he was told, was arrested; and the decision that the revolutionary tribunal was to impose the death penalty only when counter-revolutionary intent had been proved marked the end of the organized Terror. Public opinion assumed that the outcome of the Thermidor crisis meant the end of the reign of fear, and its pressure reinforced the spontaneous inclination of the deputies. In the general euphoria almost everyone found some ground for rejoicing. When Laurent Lecointre, at the end of August, denounced Billaud, Collot and Barère, together with four members of the Committee of General Security, for their share in the Terror, a chorus of indignant Montagnards silenced this imprudent reminder of the recent past.

It was not long before the unanimity arising from relief gave way to personal ambition and the remembrance of past wrongs and indignities. Former terrorists such as Fréron and Tallien made a new career for themselves as aggressive anti-Jacobins. With their encouragement, men who had been persecuted during the previous two years took over control of most of the Paris Sections, which were soon as far to the Right of the government as they had for-merly been to its Left. The trial of a batch of prisoners sent from Nantes by Carrier, one of the most ferocious of the representatives on mission, led not merely to their own acquittal but to the indict-ment of Carrier himself. In December he was sentenced to death.

As the recoil from the year II gathered momentum, the imprisoned Girondin deputies were allowed to resume their seats. Those of the outlawed Girondins who had survived – they included Isnard – were amnestied and allowed back in March 1795. Understandably, perhaps, they were in no mood for reconciliation and turned on their former persecutors with all their old implacable self-righteousness. When Lecointre returned to the charge in December he found a much more appreciative audience for his attack on the revolutionary government. The Convention voted to create a commission to investigate the charges against Billaud, Collot and Barère, together with Vadier, of the Committee of General Security. In March 1795 this commission persuaded the Assembly to send the four deputies for trial. A week later it formally disavowed the insurrection of 31 May–2 June 1793. When the Convention began to debate the charges against the four accused, their former colleagues came to their support. Robert Lindet in particular, perhaps the most moderate and humane member of the former Committee of Public Safety, in a six-hour speech defended the record of the revolutionary government and appealed to the Convention not to destroy its own reputation: 'Reject a policy that will lead you to send all your colleagues to the scaffold one after the other.' He pointed out the unwelcome truth that, if the Montagnards rejected the defence of the four – however implausible it might be – that they had been deceived or intimidated by Robespierre, the uncommitted majority would reject the Montagnards' plea that they themselves had been terrorized by the Committee of Public Safety, all of whose measures had been accepted by the Assembly. Reminding some of the present accusers of the deputies of their own bloody past, he appealed to all for a policy of oblivion. This led one of the resurrected Girondins to declare that he would shortly propose the arrest and trial of Lindet. By April 1795 the clock seemed to have been put back by two years.

In the meantime the economic policy of the Thermidoreans was in ruins. Their attempt to dismantle the controls of the year II, notably by abolishing the *maximum*, or control of the price of necessities, had met with a good deal of initial support, since educated people agreed that controls violated every sound economic principle, while the *sans-culottes* probably associated them with queues, rationing and high prices. Even given favourable climatic conditions, however, it would have been impossible to maintain the scale of the war effort without either rigorous controls or runaway inflation. In fact, the harvest of 1794 was poor, and a winter of exceptional severity produced the worst food shortages so far. The government had to resume requisitioning in order to keep the towns from starving, but it was now too weak to enforce its will as it had

Requisitioning grain

done in the previous year. The death rate rose sharply and the junketings of a handful of speculators and war contractors, although they made little difference to the physical suffering of the majority, served to exacerbate social tensions.

In Paris, by no means the hardest hit of the French towns, a hunger riot on 1 April 1795 provided the Assembly with a pretext for cutting short the interminable debates on the four accused deputies and ordering their deportation without a verdict. A more serious riot in the following month led to the invasion of the Convention itself and to disorders in which one deputy was murdered. Without proper organization or leadership the insurgents failed to take advantage of their opportunities and the government was eventually able to over-awe them by a show of force. This time fourteen Montagnard deputies who had come out in support of the insur-rection were arrested, six of them being later condemned to death. In Paris as a whole there were over 1,200 arrests. The 'disarming' of former terrorists deprived them of their civil rights as well as their pikes, and the leaders of the popular movement became the helpless victims of authority, picked up by the police whenever there was a threat of trouble and ruined by intermittent imprisonment. Things were much worse in the provinces where the partial collapse of authority, the shortage of food and the revival of royalism led to widespread brigandage, more or less politically inspired. In the south, organized murder gangs, often acting with the connivance of the local authorities and sometimes with that of the representatives on mission, massacred prisoners in a White Terror as gruesome as the prison massacres of September 1792.

Opposite, above The White Terror in the south: a bour-geois member of the Company of the Sun

Opposite, below The Assembly invaded and a deputy mur-dered; Prairial 1795

With things in this state and the Convention on the warpath against the Montagnards, a royalist restoration became a serious possibility. Fortunately for the republicans, the royalists were no less divided than they themselves. Aristocrats, pure royalists and constitutional monarchists could perhaps have agreed on the restoration of the fourteen-year-old son of Louis XVI. Since he would have needed a regent or a council of regency, such a solution might also have been acceptable to some of the more conservative republicans and offered a means of reuniting the country. His death in prison in June 1795 put an end to any such hopes. Within a month, an *émigré* landing at Quiberon in the west of France had been routed and a proclamation by the Pretender, the former comte de Provence, showed that he had no intention of accepting any compromise along the lines of the constitution of 1791. The *émigrés* were powerless to invade France; the country would not accept an unconditional restoration; the constitutional monarchists had no constitutional monarch to put forward. For the time being there was no alternative to the Convention.

The constitution of 1795 as the answer to Jacobinism

The Assembly, however, was preparing its own demise. What was officially presented as a 'revision' of the constitution of 1793 – it was, in fact, a new constitution – was voted in August. Intended to safeguard the country against both Jacobinism and royalism, the constitution of 1795 divided executive power between five Directors, who were to be chosen by the legislature. There were two Chambers, elected on the same basis and differing from each other only in the age of their members. One-third of the deputies and two of the Directors were to be changed every year. Although all those who paid direct taxation were entitled to vote in primary elections, they could only choose as electors men of substantial means. There were about thirty thousand electors and it was they who chose the deputies. This was a considerable retreat from the democratic principles of the constitution of 1793 but still revolutionary by contemporary European standards. To guard against a possible royalist victory at the polls, which would have endangered the lives of hundreds of regicide deputies, the Convention voted that two-thirds of the members of the first legislature should be taken from its own ranks.

A referendum gave a substantial majority in favour of the new constitution, which all shades of opinion were hoping to exploit to their own advantage; but it revealed much opposition to the two-thirds rule – which would prevent any of them from such exploitation in the immediate future. Royalists in Paris profited from their control over many Sections to launch an insurrectionary movement whose strength showed that they had a good deal of popular support. Its failure was due, not to any reaction by the *sans-culottes*, but to the efficiency with which Barras and Bonaparte, with the help of five thousand regular troops, organized the defence of the Assembly.

The insurgents lost about three hundred killed, which made this one of the bloodiest of the revolutionary *journées*. In a way it symbolized the combination of political weakness and military strength that characterized the revolutionary government from 1794 to 1799. Repression was significantly milder than it had been in the case of the food riots of the previous spring. The threat from the Right did, however, lead to the release of those who had then been arrested for political offences.

The constitution of 1795 ensured that the Directory would be a weak government. It tried to apply liberal policies in a situation where war, inflation, food shortages and the whole violent legacy of the Revolution made liberal government impossible. It has found few supporters, and historians have been reluctant to recognize either the achievements of these able men or the extraordinary problems that defeated them. They achieved outstanding military successes, but the country was ungovernable by normal constitutional means.

The armies of the Thermidorean Convention had overrun Holland and forced Prussia and Spain out of the war. The annexation of Belgium, however, prevented any easy settlement with the Habsburg Empire or Great Britain. The campaigns of 1796 and

The defeat of the royalist insurrection of Vendémiaire 1795

'Liberated' Holland

1797 saw the French armies win their most decisive victories of the century in Germany and Italy. With his capital in danger the Habsburg Emperor, Francis II, was forced to make peace, surrendering Lombardy and agreeing to the French occupation of the Rhineland in return for the annexation of Venetia. By 1798 a string of 'sister-republics' – in other words, puppet-states – covered France's entire eastern frontier from Holland to the Mediterranean, with a rather precarious extension through the Papal States and Naples down to the tip of Italy. The Directors themselves would have preferred a less ambitious policy in Italy and the surrender of Italian territory to buy a lasting peace with the Habsburgs, but since

Bonaparte had provided them with their most spectacular victories he was able to enforce his own terms. France was still at war with Great Britain, but a Franco-Spanish alliance forced the British to evacuate Corsica and withdraw their fleet from the Mediterranean. Although the French attempt to invade Ireland in 1797 was a fiasco, the British naval mutinies of 1797 and the Irish revolt of the following year considerably reduced the threat from across the Channel. The Directory could reasonably hope that the British would eventually have to accept the French annexation of Belgium

The Revolution on horseback: Bonaparte

and come to terms. While the war lasted it had supplied the French government with about a quarter of its revenue, in the form of spoils from the conquered provinces, and by 1797 there was at last a prospect of a return to a normal peacetime economy.

Where the war was concerned the Directory had inherited a position of strength; economically it took over a bankrupt business. Another bad harvest followed by a second hard winter administered the *coup de grâce* to the assignat. Toward the end of 1795, 8,000 million assignats were printed in a single month. A wealthy Nantes housewife, whose accounts have been preserved, had been spending roughly £15 a month at the end of 1794; a year later her monthly expenditure on bread alone had risen to over £800 and she gave up her attempts at household budgeting. In February 1796 the assignat was abandoned and replaced by the mandat territorial, which in turn was demonetized a year later. In 1797 two-thirds of the national debt was reimbursed in bonds for the purchase of what was left of the property of the Church and the *émigrés*. In the following year the

Celebrating the armistice of Leoben

government refused to accept the bonds for this purpose. This was, in effect, a declaration of national bankruptcy. However catastrophic for individuals, this brutal liquidation of the debt, together with the ending of the war on land, brought a partial return to stability. The collection of taxes improved when responsibility was transferred from elected local officials to agents of the central government. By 1798 the fiscal system was no more inefficient than it had been before the Revolution.

It is impossible to generalize about the state of the economy since conditions varied from one extreme to another. Land communications suffered from brigandage and the neglect of the roads since 1789; coastal shipping was exposed to British attacks. There was a shortage of both labour and capital on account of the war and a general reluctance to invest when conditions were so unstable. Despite the unsettling consequences of inflation, there were signs of a return to the pre-revolutionary level of activity. The Anzin mines, for example, which had produced 300,000 tons of coal a year before the Revolution and had fallen to 65,000 in 1794, were back at 248,000 by 1799. By comparison with the rapid expansion taking place in Great Britain at the same time, the recovery of lost ground still meant a relative regression – but it was better than nothing. Some industries could hope to find new markets in the conquered territories, but the outlook for overseas trade was black indeed. The Atlantic ports, the most dynamic sector of the economy in 1789, were strangled by blockade and it was not until long after the Napoleonic wars that they recovered their pre-Revolutionary activity. The Directory has often been described as a bourgeois régime and it did, on the whole, represent property rather than birth or numbers. But although it set the country on the road to recovery it was never able to do enough to satisfy either the businessmen or the landowners on whom its electoral support depended.

The Achilles heel of a regime that has been described as 'a board of executors for the revolutionary settlement' was the political legacy of the Revolution itself. Its vital problem was to retain the political support necessary for that settlement to survive. The Convention, even when the Thermidoreans had been proscribing many of its former leaders, had shown some residual solidarity. Despite its savage internal divisions, there were limits beyond which it would not go. The constitution of 1795, which involved annual elections from 1797 onward, could only provide stability if the electorate would endorse the conservative republicanism to which both principle and self-preservation bound the former members of the Convention. If the electorate opted for royalism, in any of its forms, or the extreme republicanism of the fallen Montagnards, the two-thirds rule would only protect the *conventionnels* for a few years.

Babeuf

Putting it another way, a constitution that reflected the opinions of the country was bound to provide a legislature as divided as the country itself. When this happened the men of Thermidor would only be able to maintain order by violating the constitution.

The unsuccessful insurrection of 1795 at first checked the swing to the Right by reminding the new government of the strength of royalism in Paris. The Directory therefore purged its civil service and promoted reliable republicans. As soon as the repressive hand of the government was lifted the former Jacobins began to revive. In Paris their headquarters was the new Panthéon club, which enrolled two thousand members by the end of 1795. The new Jacobinism had a pronounced social – if not yet socialist – character that was liable to frighten conservative republicans into the arms of the royalists. The Directors therefore sent Bonaparte to close the Panthéon club, together with one or two royalist clubs, in February 1796. After this demonstration that neo-Jacobinism would not be allowed to progress far by constitutional means, Babeuf, its most active exponent, went underground and began preparing for the forcible seizure of power. Babeuf's egalitarianism was of a more radical kind than any of the policies that had been aired in the year II, in the sense that it involved abolishing the private ownership of the means of production. This did not commend it either to the *notables* or to many *sans-culottes* (who thought of themselves as men of property in a small way). Babeuf's conspiracy therefore involved the creation of an elaborate 'front' organization whose members would be unaware of the ultimate aims of the leaders. The whole enterprise was a desperate affair that never amounted to much of a threat to the government. The Directors were reasonably well informed about what was going on and in May 1796 they had the leaders arrested. Their trial was a protracted business, with the government giving the conspiracy more publicity than it merited in order to emphasize the threat of anarchy. In the end Babeuf and his associate, Darthé, were shot and seven others deported.

The first major test of the new regime came with the elections in the spring of 1797. Possibly helped by the government's exploitation of the Babeuf plot, the royalists made a good deal of headway and seemed likely to win an overall majority at the next election. Although the republicans remained in control of the legislature, many local authorities were in royalist hands and the result was an influx of *émigrés* and refractory priests, in anticipation of the royalist restoration to which they hoped to contribute. The religious issue was still of prime importance to much of the population, and the Directory was unable to arrive at any tenable religious policy. The country remained predominantly Roman Catholic and the Catholic clergy were predominantly royalist. The policy of religious neutrality

The execution of the Babouvistes, 1796

attempted by the Thermidoreans therefore broke down. The Directors had not the authority, and perhaps not the cynicism either, that later allowed Bonaparte to escape from the dilemma by striking a bargain with the Pope. Their attempt to provide a substitute for Catholicism, in the form of the cult of theophilanthropy, made few converts; and they themselves were curiously indifferent toward their potential allies, the 'constitutional' clergy who were trying to reconcile the claims of God and the Republic. Their religious predicament contributed to their political dilemma; far from settling down, the country was opting for a new trial of strength.

Rather than wait for the next elections, three Directors – Reubell, La Réveillière-Lépeaux and Barras – resorted to force. On 3 September 1797, with the help of Augereau (who was

167

loaned to them by Bonaparte from the army of Italy) they bullied the legislature into deporting the other two Directors and fifty-three of the deputies. The elections in about half of the Departments were annulled. This *coup d'état* of Fructidor was followed by a partial return to the methods of the Terror. Refractory priests and *émigrés* were ordered out of the country again. Over a hundred *émigrés* were shot and 1,800 priests deported. It looked as though the only way to deal with the royalists was by reactivating the Revolution.

The government's offensive against the royalists of every persuasion produced another Jacobin revival. In the provinces, even more than in Paris, the politically active – and there were still a surprising number of them, in spite of all the deceptions of the past years – were divided into two camps. Any upsurge of the various kinds of royalists involved the persecution of the various kinds of Jacobins, and vice versa. Fructidor brought the old hands of the year II back into office in many places. The Directory, which had no intention of jumping out of the royalist frying-pan into the Jacobin fire, began to fear that the elections of 1798 would prove as embarrassing as those of the previous year, though for the opposite reason. For the first time the government made a serious attempt to 'manage' the elections, by propaganda, the suppression of opposition newspapers and the use of its agents to press the claims of officially approved candidates. It was late in reacting, however, and inexperienced in this kind of business, with the result that some of its less well-informed agents in the provinces were still trying to rally support against the royalists.

The elections of 1798 were less threatening to the government than those of the previous year. About half the new deputies could be relied on to support it; the remainder were mostly Jacobins, though there were a few royalists. The newcomers, however, included two men who had served on the Committee of Public Safety in the year II: Lindet, who might have been acceptable, and Barère, who had managed to escape whilst being deported in 1795. Rather than face such formidable opponents, the Directors and the legislature invalidated 106 of the elections. This time there was no resort to force. The means used were technically legal, but the result demonstrated once again that there was no majority in the country for the government's interpretation of the revolutionary settlement. The Directory was trying to do more than merely perpetuate itself, but stability had become identified with its self-preservation, and all chances of the new constitution's striking root had disappeared.

The next year saw the return of the two scourges which had driven the Revolution into violent courses so often before: food shortage and military defeat. The regime might have survived the poor harvest of 1799 but for the resumption of the war, which meant a return to

Bonaparte's ignominious departure from Egypt

the requisitioning of food, a shortage of credit and a sharp rise in prices. The immediate occasion for the new outbreak of fighting was Bonaparte's irresponsible invasion of Egypt, itself partly due to the weakness of a government that had been glad to get him out of the way. Bonaparte's initiative brought Russia into the war when he captured Malta from the Knights of St John, whose Grand Master was the Czar, and encouraged Austria to join in the new alliance. The more exposed of the French-controlled republics in Italy fell apart; Austro-Russian forces took the offensive in Switzerland; and an Anglo-Russian expedition landed in Holland. The situation, from the French point of view, was a good deal less serious than it looked, largely because of the disunity of the Allies, and the French armies had the situation in hand on all fronts before Bonaparte returned to France from Egypt in October. The initial reverses had nevertheless helped to discredit the regime.

In the legislature the Jacobins were joined by former supporters of the government, disconcerted by military defeat. When Reubell's term of office expired in May 1799 he was replaced by Sieyès, who was known to favour a revision of the constitution. Sieyès used the coalition of Jacobins and malcontents to force the resignation of two of his colleagues, Merlin and La Réveillière. Conscription set off a new wave of dissent that the royalists tried, without much success, to exploit for their own purposes. The royalist threat, like the danger of foreign invasion, had been mastered by the autumn, but the government was more isolated and the country farther from stability than ever.

Sieyès thought that the revision of the constitution was the only way to give the executive the power to govern. This would involve yet another *coup d'état*, for which he needed the help of a general. When Joubert, his first choice, was killed in action, the return of Bonaparte, whose prestige as the hero of the Italian campaign was undimmed by his recent failure in distant Egypt, seemed providential. Bonaparte, however, while quite prepared to overthrow the Directory, had no intention of doing it in anyone's interest but his own. Sieyès foresaw the outcome but had to accept Bonaparte's terms. The crisis broke on 18 Brumaire. On the following day (11 November 1799) the lower Chamber, in a last spasm of republicanism, refused to vote for its own destruction and its deputies were dispersed by Bonaparte's troops, who had been given to believe that their general's life was in danger. The upper Chamber and a small minority of the lower then agreed to transfer power to three consuls, one of whom was Bonaparte.

Ten years of revolution had exhausted the country, and most people were disillusioned with politicians of every colour. What decided Bonaparte's victory was not so much the success of the *coup d'état* itself as its favourable reception by public opinion at large. There was not much left that seemed worth fighting for, and people were not to know that their acceptance of Bonaparte meant that the fighting would go on and on.

Sieyès comes into his own at last

Bonaparte's *coup d'état*

Conclusion

The French Revolution has been a fertile source of myth, and much of what it symbolizes for the general public is as untrue as the familiar story of Marie Antoinette saying, 'If they have no bread, let them eat cake.' It did not do away with the Bourbons: they were back in 1814 and, if they finally lost the throne sixteen years later, it was through the folly of Charles X, the former comte d'Artois. The Revolution did not drown France in blood: the total number executed in the whole country during the terrible year II was similar to the number that fell at Waterloo in a single day. Although the actual figures will never be known, it is likely that more people were put to death after the liberation of France in 1944. Judicial murder should not be quanti-fied, but things must be kept in proportion. By twentieth-century standards the bloodshed was on a limited scale.

The Revolution did not exterminate the nobility; it did not even expropriate them. Noble birth excited suspicion and made a man more likely to be arrested, but it was never a crime in itself. Some distinguished families suffered very heavy casualties but, of the 14,000 victims of the Terror and civil war whose social origin is known, only 1,158 were nobles. About 16,000 more nobles fled the country and found their property liable to confiscation, but their ingenuity was often able to circumvent the law. After the Restoration the wealthiest men in France remained, as they had always been, noble landowners. Many bourgeois succeeded in making careers for themselves that would not have been possible before the Revolution, but neither under Napoleon nor the restored Bourbons did the middle class exercise any significant degree of political power. The distortion of economic life arising from inflation and twenty years of war favoured a few individuals but retarded industrial development as a whole, besides ensuring that influence and prestige would be monopolized by the military whose values and way of life were essentially aristocratic.

To suggest that the Revolution gave the land to the peasants is almost equally misleading. They already owned about a third of it in 1789 and, although no accurate calculations are possible, they do not seem to have gained very much of what the Church and the émigrés had lost. Landowners, rich and poor, benefited from the abolition of the tithe, and village communities as a whole were relieved of many irksome and some oppressive manorial obligations. There was perhaps more land available to rent, but it was the landowner who took the lion's share of whatever profit was available. The decline in rural violence after the Revolution suggests that conditions had become easier, but this may have been largely due to the easing of demographic pressure on the land.

In terms of who owned what, the Revolution produced many personal triumphs and some catastrophes, but nothing that could be described as a transfer of the ownership of the means of production from one class to another. At most, the process by which successful townsmen bought their way into landed society had been accelerated and the more prosperous peasants had gained in wealth and self-respect.

The importance of the Revolution lies elsewhere. Its consequences to the life of France were immense but difficult to define with precision. As the men of the time realized when they invented the expression *ancien régime*, the Revolution put an end to a way of life. The old order implied divine-right monarchy, an autonomous Church actively involved in the administration of the country and a hierarchical society in which government was a matter of negotiation about precedents between royal Ministers and the various corporate bodies whose composition and claims were the living embodiment of tradition. For a society of Orders and a kingdom of provinces the Revolution substituted a unified state where property counted for more than birth or numbers, though birth still conferred respect and property in sufficient quantity always had done. Law was henceforth codified principle rather than local custom. The political legacy of the Revolution was constitutional government and an open society where rules, at least in theory, were the same for all. For the first time it was possible to think of the country as a nation-state. Henceforth the monarchy had to govern by consent if it was to govern at all and only the Bonapartes were autocrats. Until the Revolution, the government and society of France had shared some of the characteristics of Great Britain and some of those of the despotic monarchs and stratified societies of central and eastern Europe. Throughout the nineteenth century France and Great Britain were liberal states, radically different from Austria, Prussia and the Russian Empire.

Unlike England, however, France was a country where tradition had come to a stop and the appeal to the past was a source of discord rather than of harmony. Many old attitudes admittedly persisted and spanned the revolutionary gap. The centralized pattern of Bourbon administration, which also became part of the Jacobin heritage, has lasted to the present day, and a pre-revolutionary tendency to cultural chauvinism was reinforced by the conviction of the republicans that

France was once again showing the way to everyone else. In spite of all this, much was swept away and the new framework was more a repudiation of the past than an extension of it. One consequence has been the persistent strength of extremes in a country which has still not digested the Revolution. The weakness of the divided centre that crippled the Directory has plagued much of subsequent French history. Another result has been to make France a country of paradox. Since the Revolution it has been both more and less aristocratic than England. Tocqueville saw this when, commenting on the evolution of the word 'gentleman' in England and North America, from the description of a social category to a mere form of politeness, he noted that in France *gentilhomme* dropped out of general use after the Revolution, since it still implied a qualitative distinction between different kinds of people that continued to be felt even though it was no longer mentioned. The French middle class was already frightened of what it considered to be socialism even before a belated industrial revolution had created a proletariat of any importance. Memories of the year II and the year III were etched deep and too many people had old scores to settle and old wrongs to avenge. Nineteenth-century France was both very Catholic and very anti-clerical and this was not simply another form of class antagonism. The man who read Voltaire while his wife and daughters went to church was peculiarly French. Much of what came to be regarded as typically French was in fact the product of a Revolution that left the country with a broken past.

It was the Revolution that reversed the stereotypes of England and France. Formerly England had been the land of social conservatism, bold speculation and ferocious political faction, while in France, as Beaumarchais said, *Tout finit par des chansons*, and government was always a matter of compromise. Nineteenth-century France was both socially very conservative and almost impossible to govern. Perhaps this is simply to say that successful revolutions produce stable societies, and that the French were following the British pattern a century or so later. But the French Revolution, unlike the British, has survived in the historical consciousness of the people as a whole. Where else could a newspaper ask its readers if 13 May 1958 (the date of the revolt of the Algerian settlers) was 18 Brumaire? This awareness of the Revolution as a kind of national myth is part of the air that Frenchmen breathe. It imposed itself in 1848 and again in 1871. The Vichy government of 1940 set out to exorcise the awkward ghost by the pathetic substitution of *Travail, Famille, Patrie* for that rather more inspiring triad: *Liberté. Egalité. Fraternité.* The Free French forces prided themselves on having inherited *l'esprit '89*; they were not so sure about *l'esprit '93*. One can translate *la Révolution notre mère* into English, but it does not make sense in English terms.

There is more to it than that. The Revolution was a world event and not merely an episode, however important, in the history of France. Before 1789 the statesmen of the great Powers had occasionally had to deal with peasant revolts or outbreaks of urban rioting but not with revolutionary movements in the modern sense. Henceforth the threat was always present to their imaginations and sometimes outside their windows. The French revolutionaries appealed, not to the rights of a particular past, but to universal principles they believed common to all men. It was this that so shocked Edmund Burke – and excited his distinguished contemporary, Kant. As legend, symbol and myth, the French Revolution was the affair of everyone. This was not because the French had abolished their internal customs barriers or the hunting rights of their seigneurs. What caught the imagination of Europe and the Atlantic world, whether as an inspiration or a warning, was something much simpler and more universal. Put in one sentence, it was the claim of a people's right and ability to liquidate its past and provide itself with the constitution, laws and institutions that it believed to correspond to its needs.

Perhaps this is no longer true. Outside France, 1917 may have displaced 1789, in which case something will have been lost. Even in France itself the old symbols may be giving way to new. The students in 1968, unlike the settlers in Algeria ten years earlier, looked elsewhere for their inspiration. Whatever the future brings, however, the Revolution will always remain one of the great milestones in the history not merely of France, but of the world.

Revolutionary religion makes few converts. Voltaire and Rousseau are its patron saints but the pulpit and crucifix have a more enduring look

Chronology

PUBLICATIONS

1748	Montesquieu: *De l'esprit des lois*
1749	First volume of *Encyclopédie*
1758	Voltaire: *Candide*
1760	Rousseau: *Nouvelle Héloïse*
1762	Rousseau: *Contrat Social*
1776	Adam Smith: *The Wealth of Nations*

EVENTS

1774	Accession of Louis XVI
1774–76	Turgot, Controller-General
1776–81	Necker in charge of finances
1778	France enters War of American Independence
1783	End of War of American Independence
	Calonne, Controller-General
1787	February: Meeting of the Assembly of Notables
	April: Dismissal of Calonne
	Appointment of Loménie de Brienne
	May: Dissolution of Assembly of Notables
1788	May: Judicial reforms reducing power of Parlements by Lamoignon
	June: Revolt in Grenoble
	August: Convocation of Estates General
	Recall of Necker
	December: Doubling of number of Third Estate deputies
1789	April: Riots in Paris
	5 May: Opening Session of Estates General
	17 June: Third Estate assumes title of National Assembly
	20 June: Tennis court oath
	23 June: Louis XVI announces programme of reform
	11 July: Dismissal of Necker

12 July: Riots in Paris
13 July: Formation of National Guard
14 July: Fall of Bastille
16 July: Recall of Necker
July-August: *Grande Peur*
4-11 August: Abolition of feudal rights and privileges
26 August: Declaration of the Rights of Man
5 October: March of women of Paris to Versailles
6 October: Return of king to Paris
2 November: Secularization of Church lands
December: Introduction of Assignats

1790   Civil Constitution of the Clergy
Division of Paris into 48 sections
14 July: Fête de la Fédération
August: Crushing of Nancy mutiny
September: Resignation of Necker

1791   April: Death of Mirabeau
20 June: The king's flight to Varennes
17 July: Shooting by National Guard at crowd during Champ de Mars meeting
27 August: Declaration of Pilnitz
13 September: The king's approval of Constitution
30 September: Dissolution of Constituent Assembly
1 October: First session of Legislative Assembly

1792   20 April: France declares war on Austria
13 June: The king's dismissal of Girondin ministers
20 June: Armed demonstration invades Tuileries
11 July: 'La Patrie en danger'
       Duke of Brunswick's manifesto
10 August: Constitution of the Insurrectionary Commune of Paris
       Attack on Tuileries
23 August: Prussian capture of Longwy
2-6 September: Prison massacres
20 September: French victory at Valmy
       Dissolution of Legislative Assembly
21 September: First session of Convention
22 September: Abolition of monarchy

November: Annexation of Savoy and Nice

19 November: Decree offering assistance to revolutionary movements in Europe

10 December: Beginning of king's trial

1793   21 January: Execution of Louis XVI

1 February: Declaration of war on England and Holland

25 February: Food riots in Paris

7 March: Declaration of war on Spain

March: Revolt in Vendée

9 March: Creation of Revolutionary Tribunal

6 April: Creation of Committee of Public Safety

May: Revolt of Lyons

4 May: Fixing of maximum prices for flour and grain

31 May: Rising against the Girondins

2 June: Arrest of Girondin deputies

24 June: Constitution of 1793 voted by Convention

13 July: Assassination of Marat

17 July: Abolition of remaining seigneurial rights

27 July: Robespierre's election to Committee of Public Safety

23 August: *Levée en masse*

27 August: Surrender of Toulon to British

4–5 September: Demonstration of *sans-culottes*

17 September: Law of suspects

29 September: Price and wage controls

5 October: Adoption of Republican calendar

9 October: Recapture of Lyons by Republicans

YEAR II

16 October: Execution of Marie-Antoinette

17 October: Ceremony of Reason in Notre-Dame

4 December: Law of 14 Frimaire centralizing work of Revolutionary Government

Defeat of main Vendean army

1794   March – Germinal: Executions of 'Hébertists'

April – Germinal: Executions of 'Dantonists'

8 June – 20 Prairial – Festival of Supreme Being

10 June – 22 Prairial – reorganization of revolutionary justice

26 June: Victory at Fleurus

27 July: Arrest of Robespierre, Saint-Just and Couthon

1 August: Revocation of law of Prairial

YEAR III

1794   12 November: Closing of Jacobin Club
8 December: Release of Girondin deputies
24 December: Abolition of wage and price controls

1795   April and May – Germinal and Prairial – Popular discontent and food riots
5 April: Peace with Prussia
31 May – 12 Prairial – Suppression of Revolutionary Tribunal
22 August – 5 Fructidor – New constitution

YEAR IV

1795   1 October: Annexation of Belgium
5 October – 13 Vendémiaire – Suppression of Royalist insurrection
31 October – 9 Brumaire – Election of Directory

1796   March: Bonaparte General-in-chief of the Army of Italy
May: Babeuf conspiracy
10 May: Bonaparte's victory at Lodi over Austrians

1797   Foundation of Theophilanthropy cult
18 April: Peace treaty of Leoben
9 July: Proclamation of Cisalpine Republic
4 September – 18 Fructidor – anti-royalist *coup d'état*

YEAR VI

1798   May: Bonaparte's departure for Egypt

YEAR VII

1799   May: Sieyès a Director
9 November – 18 Brumaire – *coup d'état.* Bonaparte commander of army in Paris
19 Brumaire – election of Bonaparte, Sieyès and Ducos as consuls

Bibliography

The list of books that follows has been prepared chiefly for those who wish to explore particular aspects of the Revolution in greater depth. The sheer volume of material (several hundred items on the Revolution are published each year) must mean that any short selection is based on principles rigorous enough to exclude 99 per cent of what has been published. It has therefore seemed most useful to concentrate here on more recent books and articles, some of which will not yet have been cited in other bibliographies. For a more substantial selection the reader is referred to J. Godechot, *Les Révolutions, 1770–98* Paris 1963; G. Walter, *Répertoire de l'Histoire de la Révolution française*, 2 vols. Paris 1941–45; and A. Martin and G. Walter, *Catalogue de l'Histoire de la Révolution française*, 4 vols. Paris 1936–55.

Abbreviations of titles of periodicals

AHR   *American Historical Review*

AhRf   *Annales historiques de la Révolution française*

Bull.   *Bulletin of the John Rylands Library*

EHR   *English Historical Review*

FHS   *French Historical Studies*

JMH   *Journal of Modern History*

P&P   *Past and Present*

RHes   *Revue d'Histoire économique et sociale*

RHmc   *Revue d'Histoire moderne et contemporaine*

General histories of the Revolution

R. C. Cobb *The Police and the People* London 1970

A. B. Cobban *The Social Interpretation of the French Revolution* London 1964

F. Furet and D. Richet *La Révolution* 2 vols. Paris 1955–56; English translation (abridged) London 1970

N. Hampson *A Social History of the French Revolution* London 1963

G. Lefebvre *La Révolution française* Paris 1951 (rev. ed.); English translation 2 vols. London 1962, 1969
Les Thermidoreans Paris 1937; English translation London 1965
Le Directoire Paris 1937; English translation London 1965

G. Lewis *Life in Revolutionary France* London 1972

J. McManners *The French Revolution and the Church* London 1969

A. Mathiez *La Révolution française* 3 vols. Paris 1922; English translation London 1922

R. R. Palmer *The Age of the Democratic Revolution* 2 vols. Princeton 1959, 1964

J. Roberts *French Revolution Documents* vol. 1 Oxford 1966

G. Rudé *The Crowd in the French Revolution* Oxford 1959
Revolutionary Europe London 1964

M. J. Sydenham *The French Revolution* London 1965

The *ancien régime* and the origins of the Revolution

Books

C. B. A. Behrens *The Ancien Régime* London 1967

J. F. Bosher *French Finances, 1770–1795* London 1967

R. C. Darnton *Mesmerism and the end of the Enlightenment in France* Cambridge, Massachusetts 1968

J. Egret *La Pré-Révolution française* Paris 1962

F. L. Ford *Robe and Sword: the regrouping of the French Aristocracy after Louis XIV* Cambridge, Massachusetts 1953

R. Forster *The Nobility of Toulouse in the Eighteenth Century* Baltimore 1960
The House of Saulx-Tavannes Baltimore 1971

P. Gay *The Enlightenment: an Interpretation* 2 vols. New York 1966, 1969

N. Hampson *The Enlightenment* London 1968

O. Hufton *Bayeux in the late Eighteenth Century* Oxford 1967

G. Lefebvre *1789* Paris 1939; English translation *The Coming of the French Revolution* Princeton 1947

J. McManners *French Ecclesiastical Society under the Ancien Régime. A Study of Angers* Manchester 1961

J. Mackrell *The Attack on Feudalism in Eighteenth-Century France* London 1973

G. T. Mathews *The Royal General Farms in Eighteenth-century France* New York 1958

D. Mornet *Les Origines intellectuelles de la Révolution française* Paris 1933

R. R. Palmer *Catholics and Unbelievers in Eighteenth-century France* Princeton 1939

M. Vovelle *La Chute de la Monarchie, 1787–92* Paris 1972

Articles

C. B. A. Behrens 'Privileges and Taxes in France at the end of the Ancien Regime' *Economic History Review* 1963

M. Bordes 'Les Intendants éclairés à la fin de l'ancien régime' *RHes* 1961

R. C. Darnton 'The Grub Street style of Revolution: J. P. Brissot' *JMH* 1968
'The High Enlightenment and the Low Life of Literature in pre-revolutionary France' *P&P* 1971

W. Doyle 'The Parlements of France and the Breakdown of the Ancien Régime' *FHS* 1970
'Was there an Aristocratic Reaction in pre-revolutionary France?' *P&P* 1972

R. Forster 'The Noble Wine-Producers in the Bordelais in the Eighteenth Century' *Economic History Review* 1961
'Obstacles to Economic Growth in Eighteenth-century France' *AHR* 1970

A. Goodwin 'Calonne, the Assembly of the French Notables of 1787 and the Origins of the "Révolte Nobiliaire"' *EHR* 1946
'The Social Origins and Privileged Status of the French Eighteenth-century Nobility' *Bull.* 1965

N. Hampson 'The "Recueil de Pièces intéressantes pour servir à l'Histoire de la Révolution en France" and the Origins of the French Revolution' *Bull.* 1964

M. Hutt 'The Curés and the Third Estate; the Ideas of Reform in the Pamphlets of the French Lower Clergy in the Period 1787–89' *Journal of Ecclesiastical History* London 1957

C. Lucas 'Nobles, Bourgeois and the Origins of the French Revolution' *P&P* 1973

G. V. Taylor 'Types of Capitalism in Eighteenth-century France' *EHR* 1964
'Non-capitalist Wealth and the Origins of the French Revolution' *AHR* 1967

26

THE TRANSFORMATION OF FRANCE UNDER THE CONSTITUTIONAL MONARCHY: 1782–92

Books

P. Dawson *Provincial Magistrates and Revolutionary Politics in France, 1789–1795* Cambridge, Massachusetts 1972

M. Garaud *Histoire générale du Droit privé français* 2 vols. Paris 1953, 1959

J. Godechot *Histoire des Institutions de la France sous la Révolution et l'Empire* Paris 1951
La Prise de la Bastille Paris 1965

G. Lefebvre *La Grande Peur de 1789* Paris 1932

G. Michon *Essai sur l'Histoire du*

Parti Feuillant: Adrien Duport Paris 1924

J. Egret *La Révolution des Notables: Mounier et les Monarchiens* Paris 1950

M. Reinhard *La Chute de la Royauté* Paris 1969

Articles

R. C. Cobb 'The Police, the Repressive Authorities and the Beginning of the Revolutionary Crisis in Paris' *Welsh History Review* 1967

E. L. Eisenstein 'Who intervened in 1788?' *AHR* 1965; see also the discussion provoked by this article in *AHR* 1965, 1967

M. Hutt 'The Rôle of the Curés in the Estates General of 1789' *Journal of Ecclesiastical History* 1955

D. Ligou 'A propos de la Révolution municipale' *RHes* 1960

B. Rose 'Jacquerie at Davenscourt in 1791' *Tasmanian Historical Research Association* 1973

G. V. Taylor 'Revolutionary and non-Revolutionary Content in the Cahiers of 1789' *FHS* 1972

THE TERROR

Books

R. T. Bienvenu (ed.) *The ninth of thermidor: the Fall of Robespierre* London 1968

P. Bois *Paysans de l'Ouest* Le Mans 1960

M. Bouloiseau *La République jacobine* Paris 1972

F. Braesch *La Commune du 10 août* Paris 1911

P. Caron *Les Massacres de septembre* Paris 1935

R. C. Cobb *Les Armées révolutionnaires* 2 vols. Paris 1961, 1963

P. Sainte-Claire Deville *La Commune de l'an II* Paris 1946

L. Gershoy *Bertrand Barère, a reluctant Terrorist* Princeton 1962

J. Godechot *La Contre-révolution* Paris 1961

D. Gueran *La Lutte des Classes sous la Première République* Paris 1946

J. Guilaine *Billaud-Varenne* Paris 1969

N. Hampson *The Life and Opinions of Maximilien Robespierre* London 1974

M. L. Kennedy *The Jacobin Club of Marsailles, 1790–94* Cornell 1973

A. de Lestapis *La 'Conspiration de Batz'* Paris 1969

C. Lucas *The Structure of the Terror: the Example of Javogues and the Loire* London 1973

W. Markov *Die Freiheiten des Presters Roux* Berlin 1967

A. Mathiez *Un Procès de Corruption sous la Terreur: l'Affaire de la Compagnie des Indes* Paris 1920
La Vie Chère et le Mouvement social sous la Terreur Paris 1927

R. R. Palmer *Twelve Who Ruled* Princeton 1941

A. Patrick *The Men of the First French Republic, political alignments in the National Convention of 1793* Baltimore 1972

M. Reinhard *Le Grand Carnot* 2 vols. Paris 1950

B. Rose *The Enragés: Socialists of the French Revolution?* Melbourne 1965

W. Scott *Terror and Repression in Revolutionary Marseilles* London 1973

A. Soboul *Les Sans-culottes Parisiens en l'an II* Paris 1958

M. J. Sydenham *The Girondins* London 1961

J. M. Thompson *Robespierre* 2 vols. London 1935

C. Tilly *The Vendée* London 1964

G. Walter *Robespierre* 2 vols. Paris 1936, 1939

Articles

R. Andrews 'Le Néo-stoicisme et le Législateur Montagnard' in *Gilbert Romme et son Temps* (eds J. Ehrard, A. Soboul) Paris 1966

R. C. Cobb 'The Revolutionary Mentality in France, 1793–94' *History* 1957
'Quelques Aspects de la Mentalité révolutionnaire' *RHmc* 1959

A. B. Cobban 'The Political Ideas of Maximilien Robespierre during the Period of the Convention' *EHR* 1946
'The Fundamental Ideas of Robespierre' *EHR* 1948

A. Goodwin 'The Federalist Movement in Caen during the French Revolution' *Bull.* 1960

N. Hampson 'Les Ouvriers des Arsenaux de la Marine au cours de la Révolution Française' *RHes* 1961

A. de Lestapis 'Un Grand Corrupteur, le Duc du Châtelet' *AhRf* 1953, 1955

A. Patrick 'Political Divisions in the French National Convention' *JMH* 1969

JULY 1794–NOVEMBER 1799
Books

M. Dunan *Histoire Intérieure du Directoire* Paris 1950

R. Fuoc *La Réaction thermidorienne à Lyon* Lyons 1957

J. Godechot *La Grande Nation* 2 vols. Paris 1956

C. Mazuric *Babeuf et la Conspiration pour l'Egalité* Paris 1962

A. Ollivier *Le 18 Brumaire* Paris 1959

M. Reinhard *La France du Directoire* 2 vols. Paris 1956

A. Soboul (ed.) *Babeuf et les Problèmes du Babouvisme* Paris 1963

E. Tarlé *Germinal et Prairial* Moscow 1959

K. Tønnesson *La Défaite des Sans-culottes* Paris 1959

D. Woronoff *La République Bourgeoise* Paris 1972

Articles

C. H. Church 'The Social Basis of French Bureaucracy under the Directory' *P&P* 1967
'In Search of the Directory' in J. F. Bosher (ed.), *French Government and Society* London 1973

R. C. Cobb 'Note sur la Répression contre le Personnel Sans-culotte de 1795 à 1801' *AhRf* 1954
'Quelques Aspects de la Crise de l'an III en France' *Bulletin de la Société d'Histoire Moderne* 1966

2 Frontispiece: *Le Triomphe de Marat*; painting by L-L. Boilly. Musée des Beaux-Arts, Lille. *Photo Giraudon*

8 The lord of the manor visiting his tenants; print after Moreau le Jeune (1741–1814)

10 A country road; painting by J-L. Demarne called Demarnette (1744–1829). *Photo Giraudon*

11 *La Halle*, 1779; painting by N.B. Lépicié (1735–84). Collection Marquis de Ganay

View of the corn stores, Paris, designed by Le Camus de Mézières; print by Roger after Testard. Bibliothèque Nationale

2–13 The port of Bordeaux; painting by Joseph Vernet (1714–89). Musée de la Marine. *Photo Bulloz*

Foreign wares; from Restif de la Bretonne *Les Contemporaines*, Leipzig 1784

13 The poacher and his son; painting by N-B. Lépicié (1780). *Photo courtesy Cailleux, Paris*

14 Peasants by their fireside; print by J-J. de Boissieu (1736–1810). Bibliothèque Nationale

15 Monseigneur de Valras; portrait by J-B. Greuze (1725–1805). Musée de Macon

Village priest crowning girl with roses; contemporary drawing. Musée Carnavalet

16 Colonel of the Compagnie des Gardes de la Porte de Sa Majesté; print by Hoffmann, 1786. Musée de L'Armée

17 The marquis de Sourche and his family; painting by F-H. Drouais, 1758. Versailles. *Photo Bulloz*

18 Michel Gérard and his children; painting ascribed to J-L. David, 1786. Musée de Tessé, Le Mans

19 Judges and consuls of the Bourse, Bordeaux; painting by Pierre Lacour, 1786. Musée des Arts Décoratifs, Bordeaux

21 M. de Lavoisier and his wife; painting by J-L. David, 1788. Private collection. *Photo Bulloz*

22 Louis XVI receiving members of the Parlement; drawing by P. Prud'hon (1758–1823). Louvre

23 Louis XVI in his coronation robes, 1774; painting by A-F. Callet (1741–1823). Musée de Versailles. *Photo Service de documentation photographique*

25 Vegetable sellers; contemporary print. Bibliothèque Nationale

26 Allegory of the recall of Necker, 25 August 1788; contemporary print. Bibliothèque Nationale

27 Necker acclaimed, August 1788; contemporary print. Bibliothèque Nationale

28 Marie Antoinette at Versailles, 1775; gouache by T. Gautier-Dagoty. Versailles. *Photo Giraudon*

30 The Hamlet at the Petit Trianon from *Recueil des plans du Petit Trianon* by Mique. Biblioteca Estense, Modena

The Belvedere at the Petit Trianon, as above

31 The departure of the Dragoon for the American War of Independence; painting by Michel Garnier (exhibited 1793–1814). Musée Carnavalet. *Photo Bulloz*

32 C-A. de Calonne; painting by Elisabeth Vigée-Lebrun, 1784. By gracious permission of Her Majesty the Queen

33 C-A. de Calonne; contemporary cartoon, 1787. Bibliothèque Nationale

34 Estates of Burgundy, 1775; drawing by François Devosge. Bibliothèque Nationale

Allegory of the Estates of the Dauphiné, 28 October 1788; contemporary print. Bibliothèque Nationale. *Photo Giraudon*

35 Map of the salt tax (gabelles). Bibliothèque Nationale

36 The Comte de Mirabeau (1749–91) welcomed in Elysium; detail of contemporary print after Moreau le Jeune (1741–1814). Bibliothèque Nationale

37 Charles-Louis Secondat de Montesquieu; caricature drawn by Pier Luigi Ghezzi, 1729

38 Title-page of *De l'Esprit des Loix* by C-L. Secondat de Montesquieu. British Museum

Title-page of *Contrat Social* by Jean-Jacques Rousseau, 1762. British Library

39 Frontispiece of *Le Temple de Gnide* by Charles-Louis Secondat de Montesquieu, 1772; engraving by N. le Mire

40 Title-page of *L'Encyclopédie*, 1751, edited by Diderot. British Library

41 Ceremony of the Order of the Saint-Esprit, 1724; detail from painting by N. Lancret (1690–1743). Louvre. *Photo service de documentation photographique*

43 Sellers of pamphlets; popular print, late eighteenth century. Bibliothèque Nationale

44 J-J. Rousseau; coloured lithograph from *Vues des différentes habitations de J-J. Rousseau* 1819. British Library

J-J. Rousseau; contemporary print after a portrait bust. John Rylands Library, Manchester

45 Frontispiece of *Le Devin du Village* by J-J. Rousseau, Paris, 1793. British Library

47 The abbé Sieyès; anonymous cartoon. Bibliothèque Nationale

49 View of the royal glass factory at Creusot; contemporary print

50 Voltaire; detail of statue by J-A. Houdon, 1781. Bibliothèque Nationale

51 Apotheosis of Voltaire; contemporary print. Bibliothèque Nationale

52 Mesmer's animal magnetism; contemporary cartoon. Bibliothèque Nationale

53 The Salon of the Prince de Conti in the Temple; detail of the painting by Michel-Bartélémy Ollivier (1712–84). Louvre. *Photo Bulloz*

54 The Assembly of the Notables addressed by Louis XVI, 22 February 1787; contemporary print

55 *Cahier* of the Third Estate. Archives Nationales

56 Allegory on the abolition of privileges and feudal rights, August 1789; contemporary coloured print. British Museum

58 '*Down with Taxes*'; contemporary cartoon. Bibliothèque Nationale

59 The deficit; cartoon by I. Cruikshank, 1788. British Museum

60 Voting table showing double representation of the Third Estate. Bibliothèque Nationale

61 The departure of the three Estates for Versailles, May 1789; coloured print by Vion. Bibliothèque Nationale

63 The Opening of the Estates General, 5 May 1789; print by C. Monet (1732–c.1808). British Museum

64 J-S. Bailly, the first mayor of Paris; contemporary print. John Rylands Library, Manchester

65 Oath in the Jeu de Paume at Versailles, 19 June 1789; print by C. Monet (1732–c.1808). British Museum

66 Camille Desmoulins addressing the people in the Palais Royal, 12 July 1789; print by Berthault after a drawing by J-L. Prieur (1759–95)

67 Incident in the Tuileries Gardens, 12 July 1789; print by Moreau le Jeune (1741–1814)

68 The sacking of the convent of Saint-Lazare, 13 July 1789; print by Berthault after a drawing by J-L. Prieur (1759–95)

Allegory of La Fayette as commandant of the National Guard of Paris; contemporary coloured print. British Museum

69 Guns taken by the people from the Invalides, 14 July 1789; painting by J-B. Lallemand fils (1710–1803). Musée Carnavalet. *Photo Bulloz*

70–71 The siege of the Bastille, 14 July 1789; coloured print by P-F. Germain. Bibliothèque Nationale

72 The demolition of the Bastille, July 1789; contemporary print. British Museum

73 Dancing among the Bastille ruins, 1789; Toile de Jouy fabric. Musée Carnavalet. *Photo Bulloz*

74 The duc d'Orléans, known as Philippe Egalité (1747–93); painting by L-L. Boilly (1761–1845). Musée des Beaux-Arts, Lyons

A woman of quality being whipped for having spat on Necker's portrait, 1789; popular print

75 The comte d'Artois, youngest brother of Louis XVI; gouache by Alexandre Moitte (1750–1828). Musée de Picardie, Amiens

76 A landowner trying to appease an angry crowd by the offer of a meal, August 1789; contemporary print

77 Burning of châteaux during *La Grande Peur*, July 1789; contemporary print. Musée Carnavalet

78 A poacher apprehended by a gamekeeper; contemporary print. British Museum

Bribing a judge; contemporary print. British Museum

79 The abolition of privileges, 4 August 1789; contemporary

medal by N. G. Gatteaux (1751–1832). Bibliothèque Nationale

80 Allegory on the exploitation of the Third Estate by clergy and nobility; contemporary print. Bibliothèque Nationale

A new balance of the three Orders; contemporary cartoon. Bibliothèque Nationale

81 The Indulgent Father Confessor; contemporary print. Bibliothèque Nationale

83 Honoré Gabriel Riqueti, comte de Mirabeau; painting by Joseph Boze (1744–1826). Musée Granet, Aix. Photo Bulloz

84 Royalist demonstration at the palace of Versailles, 3 October 1789; contemporary coloured print. British Museum

85 Return of the people from Versailles, 6 October 1789; contemporary print. British Museum

A democrat; English cartoon, 1791. Bibliothèque Nationale

86 Fête de la Fédération, 14 July 1790; contemporary print. Musée Carnavalet. Photo Bulloz

88 Seller of pamphlets; design for the Almanack National by Ph. L. Debucourt, 1791

89 Declaration of the Rights of Man, 20–26 August 1789; contemporary print. Bibliothèque Nationale

90 Guillotine; contemporary print. Bibliothèque Nationale

91 'Sir, your officer's uniform fits me'; contemporary cartoon. British Museum

92 The Funeral Procession of the Clergy; anonymous print, 1791. British Museum

Patriotic priest swearing civil oath, 1790; contemporary print, after Villeneuve

93 Massacre of the National Guard at Montauban, May 1790; contemporary print. British Museum

96–97 The emigrés, headed by Prince Condé, marching against revolutionary France; cartoon, 1791. British Museum

99 Louis XVI facing two ways, promising both to support and to destroy the constitution; contemporary cartoon. Bibliothèque Nationale

100 Barnave facing both ways, as courtier of 1791 and man of the people of 1789; contemporary cartoon. Bibliothèque Nationale

101 The royal family, depicted as pigs, brought back from Varennes, 20 June 1791; contemporary cartoon. Bibliothèque Nationale

102 Massacre of the petitioners, Champ de Mars, July 1791; drawing by L. Lafitte. Musée Carnavalet. Photo Bulloz

103 Jacobin and Feuillant on the gallows; contemporary cartoon

104 Attack on the Tuileries, 10 August 1792; detail of painting by Jacques Bertaux (active 1792–1802). Musée de Versailles

106 The Girondiste Pierre-Victurnien Vergniaud; drawing by L. J. J. Durameau (1733–1796). Musée Lambinet, Versailles

107 The citizen soldier's farewell; print by Le Barbier l'Ainé (1738–1826). Musée Carnavalet. Photo Bulloz

109 Louis XVI donning a Phrygian cap, 20 June 1792; contemporary print. Musée Carnavalet

110 The crowd crossing the Pont-Neuf on their way to the Tuileries, 10 August 1792; con-temporary English print. Musée Carnavalet

Pétion, Mayor of Paris, doing a political balancing act; contemporary cartoon. Musée Carnavalet

111 Map of Paris at the time of the Revolution

Marching song of the Marseilles National Guard; contemporary print

112 Louis XVI taking refuge in the Assembly, 10 August 1792; drawing by F. P. S. Gérard (1770–1837). Louvre. Archives Photographiques

113 Poster advertising sale of émigré goods. Bibliothèque Nationale

114 Man and woman sans-culottes, 1792; contemporary prints. Bibliothèque Nationale

115 Call to arms, June 1792; water-colour by Lefebvre. Musée Carnavalet

116 Massacre of women at the Salpêtrière, 3 September 1792; print from Révolutions de Paris

117 Interrogation of suspects at the Abbaye des Carmes, 5–6 September 1792; coloured con-temporary cartoon. Staatsbibliothek, Berlin

118 Prussians and Austrians in retreat, September 1792; coloured contemporary cartoon. Staatsbibliothek, Berlin

119 Battle of Jemappes, 17 November 1792; detail of con-temporary print. Musée Carnavalet

120 View of the Temple; anonymous painting, end of eighteenth century. Musée Carnavalet. Archives Photographiques

Louis XVI saying goodbye to his family, January 1793; print

by T. Ryder after Dupuis. British Museum

121 Execution of Louis XVI, in the Place de la Révolution, now Place de la Concorde, 21 January 1793; contemporary English print

The widowed Marie Antoinette; painting by A. Kucharsky (1741–1814). Musée Carnavalet. *Photo Bulloz*

2–3 Army of *sans-culottes*; contemporary English cartoon. Bibliothèque Nationale

124 Bombardment of Lyons by Republican forces, 7 October 1793; German popular engraving. Bibliothèque Nationale

125 Milhaud, member of the Convention; painting of the school of David. Louvre. *Photo Giraudon*

126 Revolutionary club at Toulon, 1793; contemporary print

128 Deputies of the Convention, headed by Hérault de Séchelles, appeasing the National Guard, 2 June 1793; print by Tassaert after F-J. Harriett (active 1798–1805). Bibliothèque Nationale

129 François Hanriot, commander of the National Guard from 30 May 1793 to 27 July 1794; contemporary print. Bibliothèque Nationale

130 Maximilien Robespierre (1758–94); portrait, eighteenth-century French school. Musée Carnavalet. *Photo Bulloz*

132 Left: Fabre d'Eglantine; detail of portrait, eighteenth-century French school. Musée de Versailles. *Photo Service de documentation photographique*

Right: Saint-Just; detail of portrait by J-B. Greuze (1725–1805). Collection M. Chevrier. *Photo Bulloz*

133 Georges Danton (1759–94); drawing by J-L. David (1748–1825)

134 Robespierre; pen drawing by Persevel Grandmaison made during session of 9 Thermidor (27 July 1794)

135 Jean-Paul Marat addressing the Assembly; print after Simon. Bibliothèque Nationale

Death of Marat, 13 July 1793; contemporary print. Bibliothèque Nationale

136 Front page of the newspaper *Père Duchesne*

J-R. Hébert as Père Duchesne; from the above newspaper

137 The making of saltpetre; gouache by P-E. Lesueur (active 1791–1810). Musée Carnavalet, collection Bidault de Lisle. *Photo Bulloz*

138 A revolutionary committee, *c.* 1794; contemporary print. British Museum

A revolutionary tribunal, Lyons, 1793–94; popular print. Musée Carnavalet

139 Marie Antoinette on her way to execution, 16 October 1793; drawing by J-L. David

A revolutionary committee; contemporary drawing by L-R. Boquet. Bibliothèque Nationale

140–41 Personifications of Brumaire, Thermidor, Germinal. Musée Carnavalet. *Photo Bulloz*

142 'Festival of Reason' in Notre Dame, 17 October 1793; contemporary German engraving. Bibliothèque Nationale

A couple reunited by the efforts of the divorce judge; gouache by P-E. Lesueur (active 1791–1810). Musée Carnavalet, collection Bidault de Lisle. *Photo Bulloz*

143 Festival in honour of the Supreme Being, 8 June 1794; contemporary print. Bibliothèque Nationale

144 Playing cards published during the Revolution representing the Constitution, Mucius Scaevola, Brutus. Bibliothèque Nationale

145 Massacre at Lyons, December 1793, ordered by Collot d'Herbois; print after Bertaux. British Museum

147 Camille Desmoulins; detail of bust by Martin de Grenoble (active 1778–1804). Musée Carnavalet. *Photo Bulloz*

150 September massacres 1792; English contemporary cartoon. Bibliothèque Nationale

151 Unemployment in the luxury trade; contemporary print. Musée Carnavalet

152 Battle of Fleurus, 26 June 1794; contemporary print. Bibliothèque Nationale

Anglo-French naval battle with battleship *Vengeur* in centre, 13 Prairial, year 2 (1 June 1794). Bibliothèque Nationale. *Photo Giraudon*

154 Allegory of the Terror, with Robespierre between two guillotines; contemporary cartoon. British Museum

155 Execution of Robespierre, 10 Thermidor, year 2 (29 July 1794); contemporary print. Bibliothèque Nationale

158 Requisitioning of corn by the government, *c.* 1794; contemporary watercolour.

159 *Companion of the Sun,* counter-revolutionary active during White Terror, 1797; contemporary print. Bibliothèque Nationale

Boissy d'Anglas faced with the head of Féraud during the invasion of the Convention, 20 May 1795; painting by Tellier (active end of eighteenth century). Versailles. *Photo Giraudon*

160 Revolutionary tyranny crushed by the friends of the Constitution of the year III; print by Massol, after Quéverdo (1748–1797). Bibliothèque Nationale

161 Events of 13 Vendémiaire, year IV (5 October 1795); print after C. Monet. Bibliothèque Nationale

162 Allegory of the Batavian Republic, *c.* 1790; print after W.H. van Bork. British Museum

163 Bonaparte; print by J.J.F. Tassaert after the painting by

Andrea Appiani (1754–1817). Bibliothèque Nationale

164 Popular rejoicing at the peace of Leoben, 18 April 1797; print after Ph.L. Debucourt (1755–1832). British Museum

166 Gracchus Babeuf (1760–1797); contemporary print. Musée Carnavalet

167 Execution of Babeuf and his fellow conspirators, 20 September 1796; contemporary print. Bibliothèque Nationale

169 The Directors Barras, La Révellière-Lepaux and Reubell, September 1797; contemporary print. Bibliothèque Nationale

170 Napoleon's flight from Egypt; 1799; contemporary English cartoon. Bibliothèque Nationale

171 Emmanuel Joseph Sieyès, in the robes of a Director; contemporary print. Bibliothèque Nationale. *Photo Lauros-Giraudon*

Bonaparte's *coup d'état* of 19 Brumaire, year 8 (9 November 1799), scene at the Corps Legislatif at St Cloud; contemporary print. British Museum

172 Ball during the *Directoire* period; coloured engraving by J.F. Bosio (1764–1827)

The parvenu and the rentier, c. 1797; contemporary print. British Museum

176 Theophilanthropic sermon; contemporary print. Bibliothèque Nationale

Index

Amar, J.-B. 148
Anzin 165
Army 92, 95, 97–8, 108, 122, 136, 153
Arras 18, 20, 27, 59, 95
Artois, comte d' 62, 75, 85, 97–8, 173, 75
Artois, Estates of 20, 59
Augereau, P.-F. 168

Babeuf, F.-N. 166, 166, 167
Bailly, J.-S. 64, 82, 139, 64
Barbaroux, C.-J.-M. 112
Barère, B. 147, 156–8, 168
Barnave, A. 27, 44, 68, 100–2, 139, 100
Barras, P.-F. 161, 167
Basire, C. 146
Bastille 68, 72–3, 77, 70–3
Batz, baron de 28
Belgium 118, 124, 161
Beaumarchais, P.-A.-C. 175
Besenval, baron de 66
Billaud-Varenne, J.-N. 116–17, 134, 139, 147–8, 153–8
Blake, W. 73
Bonaparte, N. 161, 163, 166, 168, 170–1, 161, 170–1
Bordeaux 9, 37, 124, 12, 15
Bouchotte, J.-B.-N. 145
Bourdon de l'Oise 145–7
Brest 109
Breteuil, baron de 28
Brienne, Loménie de 31–4, 42, 57, 59
Brissot, J.-P. 106–8, 116, 118
Brunswick, duke of 109
Burke, E. 49, 176

Caen 59, 124, 136
Calonne, C.-A. de 28, 31–2, 42, 50, 32
Carnot, L. 24, 134, 136, 154
Carrier, J.-B. 156–7
Chabot, F. 146

Champ de Mars (*Fête de la Fédération*) 86
Champ de Mars (Massacre) 102, 102
Chaumette, P.-G. 137, 149
Cherbourg 150
Choudieu, P.-R. 149
Clavière, E. 28, 108, 129
Clergy 16, 32, 57, 59, 92–3, 106, 114, 166–8, 92
Collot d'Herbois, J.-M. 139–40, 147–8, 153, 156–8
Committee of General Security 117, 132, 134, 144, 147–9, 153, 155, 157
Committee of Public Safety 124, 126, 131, 132, 134, 136–7, 139–40, 144, 146–51, 153, 155–7
Condé 135
Condé, prince de 97
Constitutions (1791) 94, (1793) 131, (1795) 160
Corday, Charlotte 135–6
Cordelier Club 101, 114, 117, 131, 135, 144, 146–8, 153
Couthon, G.-A. 140, 150, 154–5

Danton, G.-J. 99, 102, 114, 117, 127, 131, 135–6, 139–40, 146–9, 153, 130
Darthé 166
Dauphiné 34, 54, 34
Desfieux, F. 123–4, 140, 146, 148
Desmoulins, C. 102, 114, 147–8, 147
Dechristianization 140, 146
Diderot, D. 72
Dubois-Crancé, E.-L.-A. 103
Dubuisson 146
Dumouriez, C.-F. 124, 127
Dunkirk 137
Duport, A. 90, 100
Duquesnoy, E.-D.-F. 82

Eglantine, Fabre d' 114, 131, 140, 146–9, 133

Emigrés 75, 97–8, 106–7, 114, 159, 166, 168, *96–7, 113*
England 118, 145, 161, 163
Enragés 123
Espagnac, abbé d' 28
Estates General 33–4, 54, 57–9, 62–3, *60–1, 63, 65*
Evreux 134

Fénelon, F. *36*
Ferrières, marquis de 62, 73, 75–6, 82, 97–8
Feuillants 102–3
Fleurus 153, *152*
Fosseux, Dubois de 95
Fouquier-Tinville, A-Q. 148–9, 156
Francis II 162
Frankfurt 118
Fréron, S-L-M. 156

Garat, D-J. 146–7
Girondins 106–8, 112–14, 117–18, 121–3, 126–7, 129, 135, 139, 147, 157
Guillotin, J-L. 90

Hanriot, F. 129, 139, 148, *129*
Hébert, J-R. 127, 131, 136–7, 139–40, 145–8, *135*
Hérault-Séchelles, M-J. 128
Holland 118, 161, 170, *163*

Intendants 20–1
Isnard, M. 107, 129, 157

Jacobin Club 78–9, 102, 107–8, 123, 127, 134–5, 137, 146–9, 155
Jémappes 118, *119*
Joubert, B-C. 171

Kant, E. 176

La Fayette, marquis de 84, 98, 107–9, *68*
Lameth, A. 100
Lamoignon 33
Launay, B-R. 68
Lavoisier, A-L. *21*
Le Bas, P-E-J. 155
Le Bon, J. *154*
Lebrun, P. 108, 129
Lecointre, L. 156–7
Leopold II 98

Levasseur, R. 116, 139, 144–5, 147, 153
Liberalism 48–52
Lindet, R. 157, 168
Longwy 114
Louis XIV 42
Louis XV 24
Louis XVI 24, 26, 34, 63–4, 82, 84–5, 87–8, 98, 100–1, 107–8, 112–14, 121, *22–3, 59, 99, 101, 109, 120–1*
Louis XVII 135, 159
Lyons 124, 135, 144, 153, *124, 138, 145*

Mainz 118, 124, 135
Malta 170
Marat, J-P. 24, 114, 117, 135, *134*
Maribon-Montaut, L. 146
Marie Antoinette 34, 85, 98, 101–2, 107–8, 139, 173, *29, 101, 121, 139*
Marseilles 9, 109, 124
Merlin, P-A. 170
Mirabeau, comte de 28, 64–5, 82, 100, *36, 83*
Montagnards 117–18, 123, 126–7, 129, 131, 137, 144, 153, 155, 157, 159
Montauban *93*
Montesquieu, C-L-S. de 37–44, 48, 94, *36–9*
Morris, Gouverneur 87, 102, 132

Nantes 9
Narbonne, comte de 107
National Guard 67–8, 75, 84, 91, 102, 108–9, 112, 116, 127, 129, 156
Navy 92, 95, 98, 102, 122, 136–7, 153
Necker, J. 26–8, 34, 50, 57, 61, 65, 67, 75, *26–7, 59*
Neerwinden 124
Newspapers: *Le Père Duchesne* 127, *Le Vieux Cordelier* 147
Nice 118
Normandy 135
Notables 31, 57, *54*

Orléans, duc d' *74*

Pache, J-N. 148–9
Panthéon Club 166
Paré, J-F. 146

Paris *11, 111*; Commune 112–15,
116–17, 123, 127, 129, 132, 135–7,
140, 144, 148–9; Department 127;
Sections 109, 117, 129
Parlement (of Paris) 32
Parlements 22, 25, 33–4, 42–3, 50, 54,
57
Pereira 146
Pétion, J. 102–3, 106, 109, 112, *110*
Philippeaux, P. 146
Physiocrats 48
Pope, A. 48
Prieur, C.A. 134, 136
Proli, P.J.B. 146
Provence, comte de 97, *159*
Prussia 108, 161

Quiberon 159

Reubell 167, 170, *169*
Révellière-Lépaux, La 167, 170, *169*
Rights of Man (Declaration of) 82,
88–9, *89*
Robespierre, M.I. 18, 27, 37, 46, 50,
89–90, 94, 102–3, 106, 108, 112,
114, 116–18, 121–3, 127, 129, 134,
136–7, 139, 146–50, 153–5, *130,
134, 155*
Roland, J.M. 108, 116–18
Roland, Mme 24, 139
Ronsin, C.P. 139–40, 147–8

Rossignol, J.A. 140
Rousseau, J.J. 37, 44–8, 131, *36, 38,
44–5*
Roux, J. 123, 135
Russia 170

Saint-Just, L.A. 52, 118, 121, 123,
134, 147–8, 153–5, *133*
Sans-culottes 101–2, 113, 122–4, 126–
7, *133*, 135, 137, 150, 158
Savoy 118
Sieyès, E.J. 46–7, 65, 170–1, *47, 171*
Spain 118, 161

Talleyrand, C.M. 16, 92
Tallien, J.L. 156
Theophilanthropy 167, *178*
Tocqueville, A. 175
Toulon 124, 135, 137, 144, *126*
Turgot, A.R.J. 50

Vadier, M.G.A. 157–8
Valenciennes 135
Valmy 118
Vendée 95, 124, 135, 140, 144–6
Verdun 114
Vergniaud, P.V. *106*
Versailles 59, 84–5, *29–30*
Vincent, F.N. 131, 136, 139, 147–8
Voltaire 50, 72, *36, 50–1*

Westermann, F.J. 140